Be a Person

Understanding how to build your enterprise's social presence online — Fast!

Enterprise Executive Edition

Social Computing & Social Media for Enterprises

Social Media Performance Group

Social Media Performance Group, Inc.

Mike Ellsworth
Ken Morris
Robbie Johnson

ISBN-13: 978-1463592127

Table of Contents

What is Social Media? Social Networking? Social Computing?

"Social media are online communications in which individuals shift fluidly and flexibly between the role of audience and author. To do this, they use social software that enables anyone without knowledge of coding, to post, comment on, share or mash up content and to form communities around shared interests."

Joseph Thornley, CEO of Thornley Fallis

First off, we're going to use these three terms interchangeably throughout this book — social media, social networking, and social computing — because they all really mean the same thing — online activities involving three major components:

- User Generated Content (UGC)
- Participating in online communities
- Sharing opinions and ratings with others

Most enterprises are struggling with the effects, threats, and promise of social media these days. Many are reaping huge benefits from social media. Others are dipping a toe in the water. And perhaps the majority are wondering why they care what some Twitterer had for lunch. (We don't and frankly, nobody does.)

This executive edition of the longer **Be a Person** book will begin to straighten this all out for you. It's geared toward executives and gives you a solid foundation in the strategies and the "Whys" of social media, but not so much the "Whats" of creating your enterprise's social media presence. You'll learn the rules of the social media road, how to create a social media strategy before you start using the tools — our **No Tools Before Rules**™ concept — and tips and techniques for maximizing the effectiveness of your social media use.

You may want to give the full version of **Be a Person** to your staff or those who are going to create the implementation plans for your social media efforts.

History of Social Networks

Social networks really aren't that new. Many recognize the Website SixDegrees.com, launched in late 1997, as the first social network site.[1] SixDegrees allowed users to create profiles, list their Friends and surf the Friends' lists.

---

1 See Boyd and Ellison's research paper on social networks at: **bit.ly/91Xxhn**

What's with the bit.ly stuff?

We've used a link shortener to make it easier for you to copy the links in this document by hand. Just copy **bit.ly/** and then the nonsense letters and numbers into the address bar of your Web browser.

Figure 1 - SixDegrees.com's First Main Page - First Social Network

Others point to the ancient discussion groups on USENET (begun in 1979), the pioneering online community the Well (AKA Whole Earth 'Lectronic Link — started in 1985), the communities on CompuServe (1979) and Prodigy (1988), and Internet Relay Chat (IRC — started in 1988) as early social networks.

While all these examples did indeed constitute online communities, they may not quite fit the modern definition of social networking for a variety of reasons, including the limited number of social features and the way they were integrated into the communities. However, they did fulfill our three requirements for a social network: They enabled, encouraged, and facilitated User Generated Content; they were online communities; and although sharing opinions and ratings with others was not usually formalized, commenting was generally fully supported.

So social networking has been around at least since 1979, when Duke University graduate students Tom Truscott and Jim Ellis, and Steve Bellovin, a graduate student at the University of North Carolina, created the USENET software and installed it on the first two sites: "duke" and "unc," which were connected by a relatively new network (created in 1969) called the Internet.

But in reality, you probably already belong to the oldest social network of them all: email. Electronic mail began in 1965 as a way to send messages on a mainframe computer. Modern email was invented by Ray Tomlinson, one of the forefathers of the Internet, in 1971.[2] The only one of our three social networking criteria that email doesn't obviously fulfill is: participating in online communities. If you've ever been part of an email group (AKA a listserv) or email newsletter, you know email can provide online community.

So **you** are a veteran user of social networking!

Social Sites Defined

Social networking sites will come and go, but the approaches to going social that we describe in this book can be adapted for any site. With that said, let's take a look at some of the most popular and useful social sites and concepts out there, and give some quick definitions.

[2] Read a conversation with Tomlinson: **bit.ly/d0tWEj**

Facebook

Facebook is the largest social networking site by far, with more than half a billion users. Many of its users use the site to keep up to date with friends and to "follow" celebrities, popular TV shows and movies, and businesses. However, many use Facebook for serious purposes such as recruiting talent, selling products, and creating communities around products or services.

The major features of Facebook include **friending** — connecting with other users so that you can see their activities; **posting statuses** — short blurbs about what you are doing or interested in; reading what others are posting in your **News Feed**, a constantly updating timeline of the comments and activities of your friends; and **playing online games** such as Mafia Wars and Farmville.

If you want to learn more about using Facebook, see the section *Setting Up Facebook* in the full version of **Be a Person**.

LinkedIn

LinkedIn is the most professional of the popular social networks. Users tend to be more affluent and influential, and more of their interactions involve some business purpose rather than being purely social. LinkedIn is a great place to prospect for talent, find partners and customers, and find evangelists (there's more on evangelists in the full version of **Be a Person**). LinkedIn is organized around your user profile, which is like a resume on steroids. In addition, users' profile pages feature a **News Feed** similar to Facebook's as well as any number of plug-in applications such as Reading List by Amazon, SlideShare, blogs, and others.

LinkedIn has many features that enable you to find and connect with other users, but you are limited in the number of people you can contact directly and/or connect with. LinkedIn uses a principle of three degrees of separation: those you are connected to are your first degree network; those that your connections are connected to are your second degree network; those who are connected to your second degree network are your third degree network. You can only directly contact your first degree network, but can ask those contacts for help in connecting to people in your second or third degree networks.

We explain this concept in more detail in the section *Setting Up LinkedIn* in the full version of **Be a Person**.

One of the most useful aspects of LinkedIn is their **Groups** function. Anyone can create a group and invite like-minded people to join. It's a great way to meet others who share your interests. Another useful function is **LinkedIn Answers**, which enable users to ask and answer questions on any subject.

Twitter

Twitter is what is known as a **microblogging** social network. Members post messages of up to 140 characters (known as **tweets**) and those who follow them see the messages in their **News Feeds**. Often derided as shallow, trivial, and boring, Twitter is used for talent acquisition and all sorts of business and professional functions, including organizing online and offline events, and spreading the word about products and services.

People who follow your tweets are called **followers**, and if they like a tweet they may **retweet** it — repeat it — to their followers. You can find people to follow by using the Twitter Website's search function to search for words or phrases or for special keywords called **hashtags**. Hashtags are created by putting a pound sign (#) in front of a word, for example #marketing. People do this so their tweets can be associated with others on a similar topic. For example, many recruiters post their job openings on Twitter using the hashtag #job.

Twitter is often used to call attention to a Website or a blog or other online destination. With only 140 characters to play with, it's hard to say anything complicated, and thus Twitter often serves as an advertisement for lengthier treatments of a subject.

There's more about using Twitter in the section *Setting Up Twitter* in the full version of **Be a Person**.

Twitter Directories – WeFollow, Twellow, etc.

Twitter has spawned its own universe of related sites, including many different sites dedicated to helping users find tweets and **tweeps** (people on Twitter) of interest. Directories like WeFollow and Twellow enable users to list themselves, add tags describing their interests, and use tags to search for tweeps that share their interests.

Tweetups

A tweetup is not a site, but rather an offline gathering organized via Twitter. Organizations as diverse as NASCAR,[3] NASA,[4] and non-profits such as GiveMN[5] and Maui Food Bank[6] have used tweetups. Tweetups offer a chance for people

---

[3] NASCAR Tweetups: **exm.nr/fH5zR4**

[4] NASA Tweetups: **bit.ly/hp0LXm**

[5] GiveMN Tweetup: **bit.ly/dLTwXt**

[6] Maui Food Bank Tweetup: **bit.ly/ggP0Tt**

who may only know one another virtually to meet in person. It's a great idea for enterprises because it can solidify interest and support for your products or services.

YouTube

YouTube is a free service that lets people post short videos. Users can create a **channel** to house multiple videos, and other users can subscribe to the channel, **tag** videos within it, and **comment** on them in text or by posting a video reply. In most cases, users can **embed** (insert) videos on their Websites without the poster's permission, thus providing a free source of content for their own Websites.

YouTube is largest video service of its kind, but there are lots of others. YouTube tends to be in the forefront of the social networking aspect of video, offering users ways to follow and comment on others' videos.

There's more about using YouTube in the section *Setting Up YouTube* in the full version of **Be a Person**.

MySpace

One of the oldest social networking sites, MySpace has faded with the ascendency of Facebook. The site is based around **profiles,** which are generally long, customized, crowded pages with distracting design. Still popular with bands and high schoolers, MySpace, in a bid to remain relevant, now allows users to log in with their Facebook credentials and seems to be positioning itself as a content provider and aggregator.

There's more about MySpace in the section *Setting Up MySpace* in the full version of **Be a Person**.

StumbleUpon, Delicious, Digg, Flickr

These sites are known as social bookmarking sites. Each provides ways for people to discover Websites, videos, blogs and pictures of interest based on the efforts of other users, who **tag** sites of interest with keywords that others can find via searches. StumbleUpon will email you with suggest sites in categories that you select. Delicious and Digg enable you to search for keywords as well as suggesting general interest items. And Flickr specializes in photos, enabling you to **post** and tag photos and share them with friends.

Blogs

Short for Weblog, blogs are a way to post longer-form **articles** that may include pictures and videos. The average blog post is not terribly long — perhaps 400 to 700 words — that usually treats a single subject. Some blogs are user's everyday thoughts, like a diary, and others treat technical, philosophical, or religious topics. The most popular blog site is the Huffington Post (now part of AOL), which examines political topics, but there are also popular blogs that follow celebrities (TMZ, Perez Hilton), technical gadgets (engadget, Gizmodo, TechCrunch), or post satirical takes on current events (Gawker, The Onion).

Anyone can create a blog, and tens of millions have. A blog is a particularly good way for enterprises to engage with their communities.

There's more on blogging in the section *Setting Up Blogging* in the full version of **Be a Person**.

Google Alerts, Blog Search, Reader

Google has a wealth of tools to aid you in monitoring what people are saying about your enterprise on social media sites.

Google Alerts are automated searches you can set up that will search for keywords and email you the results regularly. At the very least, your business should have some Google Alerts set up.

Google Blog Search does, guess what? Blog searches. It's another great way to keep tabs on the conversation.

Google Reader enables you to subscribe to RSS feeds (see below). Most blogs have feeds that Google Reader can consolidate into one place for you to read, sample, or skim.

RSS Feeds

Standing for Really Simple Syndication, RSS is a way for users to "subscribe" to the updates of a site or a blog. Subscribing means that whenever the content changes on the subscribed-to site, an update is made available. You can keep up with the update by subscribing to the RSS feed using an RSS feed reader, like the free Google Reader. That way you don't have to constantly revisit the site to see if anything has changed. You should consider implementing an RSS feed for your own site and social media properties.

Social Aggregators - Plaxo and FriendFeed

Started in 2002 as an address book synchronization service and purchased by Comcast in 2008 for $150 million, Plaxo added social aspects including the ability to follow multiple social media **News Feeds** from more than 30 sites (like Twitter, Yelp, Flickr, Facebook, and LinkedIn), a birthday reminder and ecard service, and user profiles. Plaxo's 20 million social members (and 50 million address book users) tend to be business-oriented. Although it's not often thought of for its social networking features, Plaxo is worth considering for use by enterprises.

FriendFeed enables social media friends to follow one another's' feeds from more than 50 social networks in one place. FriendFeed pulls friend activity from the social sites and assembles it into a **News Feed** on its site. Users can thus just check the FriendFeed without having to visit several social sites to keep up with their friends.

Location-Based Sites — FourSquare and GoWalla

With the rise of the smart phone, location-based sites have gone wild. FourSquare allows users to "**check in**" either manually or automatically at real-world locations such as bars, restaurants, and other venues. The idea is to help provide a real-world connection for social-world friends. But detractors say the information these sites provide about where people are right this moment is an invitation to burglary or worse.

You'll want to consider whether to make location-based sites part of your social media strategy.

Expert Sites — Squidoo, About.com, eHow

There are lots of expert sites on the Web. Some are heavily curated (About.com has editors assigned to most of their expert areas); some are automated (Squidoo aggregates lots of content on a single topic); others are organized around how-to areas (eHow has articles and videos that show you how to do almost anything).

You should review these sites to see if they're talking about you and your products or services, and to determine if they might include your enterprise in their materials.

White Label Sites – Ning, Jive

White label social media sites provide the tools for you to build a standalone social media site for your enterprise. One of the oldest and best is Ning ("peace" in Chinese), which hosts more than four million sites. Incidentally, cofounder and Ning chairman Marc Andreessen created the first insanely popular Web browser, Netscape, back in 1996 and sold it to AOL for $4.2 billion in 1999.

Your business can get started on Ning for a few dollars a month. Of course, first you need to know whether your community needs (another) place to go, and whether you're ready to commit to the effort necessary to create and host a community.

Jive is an enterprise-class social media and collaboration platform. Enterprises can use the software to create branded social media communities that can be used for customer support, marketing, or internal collaboration. Enterprises such as United Health Group, Nike, Cisco, and CSC are using Jive for marketing, customer communities, collaboration, and internal training.

Jive is positioned in the leaders quadrant on both the Gartner Magic Quadrant and Forrester's Wave.

Orkut and Bebo

Social media is a worldwide phenomenon, and while a large percentage of Facebook's membership lives outside the US, there are also social networks like Orkut and Bebo that focus on non-US members.

Orkut is owned by Google and has more than 100 million users. After starting as an invitation-only network in the US, its largest proportion of users now come from Brazil, where it is one of the most popular Websites, and from India.

Acquired by AOL in 2008 and then sold to hedge fund operators Criterion Capital Partners in mid-2010, Bebo was also started in the US and now has more than 40 million users, a quarter of which are from the UK.

If your enterprise wants to reach outside the borders of the US, consider using social networks such as these.

Knowem

Knowem is one of many sites that will allow you to reserve your enterprise's presence on hundreds or even thousands of social media sites. You can use the site to do this even if you have no plans to create a presence on hundreds of sites. It's a good idea because a) you may someday want to join one of the obscure sites and b) you may want to prevent others from usurping your identity on social sites.

Knowem is also a good way to research specialty social media sites where your community may have an active presence.

Social Media Badges

Many sites provide badges, little graphics that represent the site or some achievement, to supporters who then post them on their blogs or other sites. One example of this is on LinkedIn. When you join a LinkedIn group, you have the option to display the group's badge on your profile so others see you're a member.

Badges are also given by sites like FourSquare to signify some achievement or status. It's a good way to enable and encourage evangelists.

There are also other types of badges that recognize achievements of your supporters, such as "Top Blogger" or "Most Valuable Evangelist."

Why Social Media?

"One of the things our grandchildren will find quaintest about us is that we distinguish the digital from the real . . . In the future that will become literally impossible."

William Gibson, author

You're reading this book because you're at least curious about social media. You probably want to know why there's such a fuss about it, and you'd like to find out if it can help your enterprise. We'll get to all these topics, but first, why should you care at all about social media?

One reason is it is the fastest growing segment of the Internet, having recently overtaken online games and email as the most-used category of applications on the Internet.[7]

Think of how much you use email, and how much those

---

[7] Nielsen Online: **bit.ly/bkJZvx**

around you use it. People are using social networking more often than they are using email.

In fact, here are some statistics on various social media properties:

• YouTube is now 10 percent of all Internet traffic[8]	• There are 1.5 million blog posts per day (17 per second)[9]
• YouTube & Wikipedia are among the top brands online[10]	• Five of the top 10 Websites are social[11]
• There are more than 144 million blogs[12]	• More than 175,000 new blogs launch every day[13]

---

[8] Ellacoya: **bit.ly/8YKzTr**

[9] Technorati: **bit.ly/9eXgAj**

[10] BrandChannel: **bit.ly/aMurzT**

[11] Alexa: **bit.ly/dzCkL5**

[12] BlogPulse: **bit.ly/9ZOfK9**

[13] Hmmm. Apparently Technorati said this as long ago as 2008, but this seems to be an accepted bit of Web lore at this point: a stat everybody quotes, but has no findable source.

Unconvinced? How about some more statistics?

- Americans spent an average 5 hours 35 minutes a month on social networking sites in 2009
- There are more than 142 million regular users of social media and half of Facebook users log in daily
- If Facebook were a country, it would be the world's third largest,[14] with 500 million people, having overtaken the US, at 308 million[15]
- Online communities are visited by 67 percent of the global online population, which numbered 1.8 billion at the end of 2009[16]
- Nearly two-thirds of US Internet users regularly use a social network (and almost two-thirds of all Americans are on the FTC's no-call list!)[17]
- Nielsen Netview found that in 2010 social media use by Americans dwarfed other online usage by more than two-to-one (see chart on next page)

---

[14] For a light-hearted take on what this means, see: **bit.ly/aInzw2**

[15] **bit.ly/biGYNr**

[16] **bit.ly/AKbO5**

[17] Nielsen, Social *Networking's New Global Footprint:* **bit.ly/ILH53L** and Switched, *FTC's 'Do Not Call' List Hits 200-Million Mark, but Telemarketers Still Call:* **aol.it/lqY9Fh**

Figure 2 - Source: Nielsen Netview, June 2010[18]

Managed security company Network Box found in an April, 2010 survey[19] that social media sites dominate Internet usage by businesses. According to the company, employees watching YouTube videos accounted for 10 percent of all corporate bandwidth during Q1 2010 — up two percent over the previous quarter.

---

[18] Nielsen Netview: bit.ly/bKJZvx

[19] bit.ly/dBffUl

The top five bandwidth Websites, and the percentage of all bandwidth they used, were:

1. YouTube — 10
2. Facebook — 4.5
3. Windows Update — 3.3
4. Yimg (Yahoo Image Search) — 2.7
5. Google — 2.5

Business usage of YouTube and Facebook sucks up almost 15 percent of the average business's bandwidth! This brings us to another reason to be interested in social media: It's already here. Your enterprise is already dealing with its effects. You need to understand it, plan for it, and create a social media strategy for your enterprise, if only in self-defense.

And if that doesn't do it for you, consider the fact that Amazon recently was granted a patent[20] for "A networked computer system [that] provides various services for assisting users in locating, and establishing contact relationships with, other users," — in other words, social networking. When the big boys get this serious, you know something's going on.

We'll show you lots of other good reasons to be interested in social media throughout this book.

---

[20] Amazon granted a social networking patent: **bit.ly/cyB3p8**

How is Social Media Relevant to Business?

"We now have indisputable proof that online marketing, YouTube and Twitter and all that it encompasses is meaningful and has arrived. We are seeing real consequences to a mistake.
If [social networks] didn't matter, you wouldn't see this type of reaction from J&J or consumers
[over the Motrin Mom faux pas]."

**Gene Grabowski, chair
crisis and litigation practice,
Levick Strategic Communications**

Grabowski is referring to one of the entries in our Social Media Hall of Shame.[21] That entry reads as follows:

In fall of 2008, pain reliever brand Motrin posted a short video as part of an ad campaign aimed at young mothers. In an attempt to identify with its intended audience, the ad featured a young woman speaking in an irreverent tone about the "fashion" of wearing one's baby, and the back pain associated with the practice.

Some online moms found the tone patronizing and felt they were being mocked. The video went largely unnoticed for 45 days, but then on Saturday, November 15, one mother, Jessica Gottlieb, tweeted her disapproval using the Twitter hashtag[22] #motrinmoms.

By Sunday afternoon, #motrinmoms was one of the hottest hashtags on Twitter. Mommy Blogger Katja Presnal created a nine-minute YouTube video comprised of angry tweets from moms with baby carriers.[23] In all, however, fewer than 1,000 people posted using the hashtag. But this was a very vocal minority.

By social media standards, Motrin was slow to respond to the outcry. Yet by Sunday evening, they pulled the campaign, temporarily shuttered their Website, and apologized. Instead of engaging with the protestors on their own turf, however, Motrin reverted to an Old Media response: They tried to remove all traces of the video and ad campaign and offered a

---

[21] Social Media Performance Group's Social Media Hall of Shame: bit.ly/bjon3u

[22] See the definition for hashtag on page 12.

[23] The video *Motrin Ad Makes Moms Mad*: bit.ly/bZvjBR

corporate apology in response: "We have taken immediate action to respond to these concerns and have removed the advertisement from our Web site."

By November 20th, they had pulled themselves together a bit more, and published a response with a much better tone. Kathy Widmer, Vice President of Marketing for McNeil Consumer Healthcare, offered a new apology that followed our mandate: **Be a Person**.

> So...it's been almost 4 days since I apologized here for our Motrin advertising. What an unbelievable 4 days it's been. Believe me when I say we've been taking our own headache medicine here lately! We are parents ourselves and we take feedback from moms very seriously.[24]

Much, much, **much** better!

Motrin's mistake was in not using the negative attention to engage in a dialog with the angered moms. By taking them seriously and listening to their concerns, Motrin could have probably defused the uproar and possibly turned the furor into an advantage. Engaging in a dialog would have enabled Motrin to explain that they were trying to be funny, and they were sorry that hadn't worked.

Ironically, Jessica Gottlieb, author of the original tweet, said that she felt the ad did not need to be pulled. What if Motrin had originally addressed her directly and enlisted her help?

---

[24] Read more about the Motrin debacle at **bit.ly/awmztq**

We can learn two things from this object lesson:

- Social media can bring a powerful company to its knees in the space of less than a week
- With great power comes great responsibility[25]

We don't tell this tale to scare you, but rather to impress upon you the power and potential of this new communications medium. We also hope Motrin's story demonstrates that using social media without a strategy and a plan may seem easy to do, but like juggling chainsaws, the outcome is much better when you're trained and prepared.

Plenty of enterprises have produced great results through the use of social media. We've written this book to help you become one of them.

On the positive side of social media, take a look at the Blendtec YouTube videos,[26] one of the keystone case studies from our Enterprise Social Media Framework (ESMF).[27]

Blendtec makes powerful blenders, and so someone got the bright idea of doing a series of short videos called *Will it Blend?* Starting way back in 2006, and featuring Blendtec CEO Tom Dickson, each video — designated either "Try this at home" or "Don't try this at home" — blends a range of items from 50 marbles and a handful of golf balls to a new iPhone.

It was the iPhone blend video that went viral, racking up more than 9.8 million views, and counting. Combining the fetish

---

[25] Spider-Man: **bit.ly/lnBePi**

[26] Blendtec's YouTube channel: **bit.ly/ypHXin**

[27] Enterprise Social Media Framework: **bit.ly/auxUYA**

power of the game-changing mobile phone with the eccentric idea of obliterating things with a blender equated to tremendous viralocity. Since the first iPhone bit it, the company has trashed a series of iconic electronic gadgets, including an Olympus digital camera, an iPad (11 million views), and an iPhone 4.

Was it planned this way? No. It was just a wacky— and cheap— bid for attention from a small company with a small marketing budget. It went viral because . . . well, just because it was bizarre, over the top, and cool, we guess. For almost no money, Blendtec has reaped more than 161 million YouTube views, 380,000 subscribers (making it #40 on YouTube's all-time list), and a 7X increase in sales.

So why do we mention this? Did you see the part about "almost no money?"

You could go viral as well. But to do so, you must be hooked into the zeitgeist[28] of your community, and the larger society. Offbeat, quirky ideas are what generally go viral. But if you try too hard (we're looking at you, LonelyGirl15[29]) you could do more damage than good.

Contrast BlendTec's success with the fact that the #3 result from a search on YouTube for Comcast is a video called *A Comcast Technician Sleeping on my Couch.*[30]

(There's more about going viral in the full version of **Be a Person** in the section *Aim to Influence*.)

---

[28] Google zeitgeist: **bit.ly/cy2fhg**

[29] LonelyGirl15's YouTube channel: **bit.ly/dBib9J**

[30] A Comcast Technician Sleeping on my Couch: **bit.ly/jPRrHZ**

Talk about incredible results, both good and bad! Social media is here, it works for enterprises, and chances are good it is affecting your business today.

Social Media and Your Business

Now you may be thinking, "That's great and all, but my enterprise sells to businesses (or sells services, or is in a regulated industry, or . . .), and I can't see how funny YouTube videos will help me sell my product."

You're not alone in being skeptical about the potential effect of social media on your business. But more and more businesses of all sizes are starting to embrace it.

A 2011 Frost and Sullivan study[31] (see Figure 3) showed that of 200 C-level execs, 69 percent were closely tracking social media. That's amazing in and of itself, but executive interest in social media was greater than of other important technology trends, such as telepresence, VOIP, shared team spaces, soft phones, and even unified communications and unified messaging. Half of the respondents said social media is already used within their organization, and 41 percent said they were using the technology personally.

---

[31] Frost & Sullivan report: **bit.ly/l7FMin**

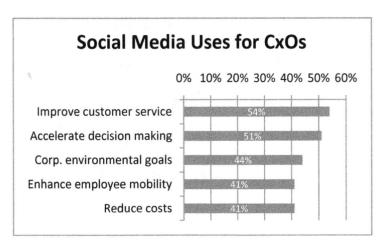

Figure 3- Frost & Sullivan Survey - Goals for CxOs Who Plan to Increase Social Media Use

Social media expert Josh Bernoff of Forrester Research, writing for the Harvard Business Review,[32] divides large enterprises' use of social media into four groups:

- **Dormant** — Fewer than one in five large companies are in this group. They haven't really gotten started with social media.

- **Testing** — About one third of enterprises are just starting out. They usually begin with listening (monitoring social chatter) and talking on Twitter and Facebook.

- **Coordinating** — Another third of large companies have moved on to coordinating multiple social efforts around the company. Bernoff recommends, and we definitely agree, that the right strategy is not to put all the social efforts under one manager. He recommends appointing

---

[32] Harvard Business Review: **bit.ly/kCuVFK**

"shepherds" to help lead social media across teams in marketing, customer support, HR, and IT.

- **Mastering** — The remainder of companies, the smallest group, have mastered social media use. They face challenges in scaling and optimizing social efforts.

Bernoff points to Dell as a leader. Manish Mehta is Dell's VP, Social Media & Community. Just having an executive position with a name like that indicates how seriously Dell takes social media.

Bernoff says Mehta "has a weekly teleconference with managers throughout the organization who are responsible for the hundreds of social applications the company deploys, from the Twitter feed @DellOutlet that promotes overstock computers to IdeaStorm, the online community that solicits ideas for new Dell products. Coordinating measurement is also key: at financial services company USAA, for example, social media managers have proven that ratings and reviews generate a 17% increase in clickthroughs to product purchase pages."

So it's early days, but despite that, many enterprises have seen real benefits from engaging with social media.

But it's not all about sales and marketing, as you can see from the preceding. In fact, we believe that sales and marketing are not even the most impressive things social media does. Savvy businesses use social media to:

- **Track what customers and prospects are saying**, what they're interested in, and how they buy
- **Create flash focus groups** online to get real-time, real-world feedback on customer likes and dislikes

- **Recruit new talent** — many companies are turning away from posting job requisitions to searching social networks like LinkedIn and inviting highly-qualified people to apply
- **Increase employee engagement**, satisfaction, and retention — McKinsey and MIT surveys found between 7 percent and 20 percent improvement in employee retention due to social networks[33]

If that's all social computing could do for your business, wouldn't that be enough?

Our contention that most businesses miss the real point and much of the potential of social media is supported by a recent white paper published by the Harvard Business Review.[34] HBR did a survey of 2,100 companies, and these were some of their findings:

> Despite the vast potential social media brings, many companies seem focused on social media activity primarily as a one-way promotional channel, and have yet to capitalize on the ability to not only listen to, but analyze, consumer conversations and turn the information into insights that impact the bottom line.

For instance:

> o   Three-quarters (75%) of the companies in the survey said they did not know where their most valuable customers were talking about them

---

[33] Allyis blog: **bit.ly/k2TD3m** and McKinsey: **bit.ly/k8hl1q**

[34] Harvard Business Review, "The New Conversation: Taking Social Media from Talk to Action" **bit.ly/I9hNpQ**

- Nearly one-third (31%) do not measure effectiveness of social media
- Less than one-quarter (23%) are using social media analytic tools
- A fraction (7%) of participating companies are able to integrate social media into their marketing activities

Only a small group — 12 percent — of the companies in the survey said they felt they were currently effective users of social media. These were the companies most likely to deploy multiple channels, use metrics, have a strategy for social media use, and integrate their social media into their overall marketing operations.

By reading this book, and using the full **Be a Person** in your organization, you can learn how to become part of the successful 12 percent.

Let's Face It

They're talking about you online (if you're lucky).

That's right, there are probably people talking about your business online right now, via social media. What are they saying? Are they supporters or detractors? Shouldn't you listen to find out?

What are people who are interested in your business talking about online?

Of course, it varies depending on the business you're in, but you can count on the chatter being both positive and negative, just like offline conversations about you. The difference is, you can join in on these conversations and possibly influence them.

Regardless of what people are saying about you, shouldn't you be aware of the online conversations? What if Motrin had ignored what the Mommy Bloggers were saying? What if people are right now, this very minute, spreading misinformation or rumors about your company on Facebook?

Wouldn't you want to know?

Social media changes the way cheers and raspberries are distributed. Two of our favorite quotes about how much social media changes positive and negative conversations come from trailblazing broadcaster Edward R. Murrow and Paul Gillin, author of The New Influencers.

> The fact that your voice is amplified to the degree where it reaches from one end of the country to the other does not confer upon you greater wisdom or understanding than you possessed when your voice reached only from one end of the bar to the other.
> — Edward R. Murrow[35]

> Conventional marketing wisdom long held that a dissatisfied customer tells ten people. But…in the new age of social media, he or she has the tools to tell ten million.
> — Paul Gillin[36]

---

[35] Edward R. Murrow at the RTNDA Convention (Radio-Television News Directors Association and Foundation) in Chicago on October 15, 1958. **to.pbs.org/Id0Mvy**

[36] Harvard Business Review, "The New Conversation: Taking Social Media from Talk to Action" **bit.ly/I9hNpQ**

Social media hasn't changed people, just as Murrow says; it has amplified their voices far beyond what Murrow imagine in 1958, to the point that mass media is accessible to the average person, as Gillin's quote demonstrates.

OK, OK, social media is the next big thing. How can you start to take advantage of it?

Well, one thing you shouldn't do is go off into this new land of social media without a map. You need to channel social media's power to support your business's strategy. To harness the power of Social Media, you need a strategy, and a plan.

So What's Your Strategy?

Like anything that's worth doing well, it's best to have a strategy for using social media. You may be tempted to listen to those in your business who have a "Hey kids! Let's put on a show!" kind of mentality regarding social media. It's so easy to get started, you may decide to listen to these folks and start creating a Facebook page, a Twitter account, or a YouTube channel right away.

We hope you will resist the temptation to jump in with both feet until you have understood why you are using social media, and how it is going to support your overall strategy.

To maximize social media benefit, you need to align your business's strategy with both your external and internal social media strategy.

The difficulty in writing a book about social media and business is that there are so many kinds of enterprises, each with unique missions and goals. We could give advice for a medical device manufacturer, for example, which may not be appropriate for grocery distributor. On the other hand, most businesses face similar challenges such as selling, marketing, recruiting and retaining employees, gaining brand recognition, and so on.

Thus you will need to take the general principles in this book and apply them to your own enterprise. Without working closely with you, we can't identify for you the best social media goals, strategies, sites, and techniques for your business. Only you can do that, and you should use your overall mission, strategy, and goals to determine your social media strategy.

There's more detail later about creating strategies. First, we'd like to lay out the general concepts, and get more specific in the chapter *Create Social Computing Strategies* on page 75.

A good social media strategy:

- Effectively communicates goals and benefits of social media internally and externally

- Guides selection of the right tools to use

- Ensures sustainability of your social media endeavor

- Involves regular reviews of people, processes, and tools to ensure that your business stays relevant

The first step is to review your business's goals and strategy. Identify the most important, and start to think how social media can help, especially in ways other than sales and marketing. Make whatever changes necessary to your strategy to bring it up to date and ensure that all stakeholders support it before taking a look at social media.

Create an Internal Social Media Strategy

It may be easier for you to start by focusing on creating an internal social media strategy. It's less scary, and you might have an easier time coming to agreement on the internal strategy. Some internal goals to think about include:

- Empower employees to advocate
- Improve employee engagement and retention
- Encourage collaboration, innovation, problem solving
- Improve communications
- Manage risk to your reputation
- Improve your hiring process
- Improve your market research

We elaborate more on this concept in the *Create an Internal Social Computing Strategy* section on page 79.

There's more information about engagement, advocacy, and evangelism in the sections *Engage Your Community*, *Find and Create Online Evangelists*, and *Create Buzz* in the full version of **Be a Person**.

Create an External Social Media Strategy

Once you understand how social media can support your business's overall strategy, it's time to create your external social media strategy.

You need to go where your community is. Identify constituent groups to target — prospects, customers, influencers, evangelists, opinion leaders — and find out if they use social media. Delve into specifics. Are they reading any particular blogs? Are they on Twitter? Facebook? Find your community and study them to see what their concerns are. We examine this process in depth in the section *Find Your Community* in the full version of **Be a Person**.

Base your strategy on what you find through this research. If your target group is on Facebook, you may want to set up a business page. If your community tweets, you may want to set up a program of daily updates on Twitter.

If you haphazardly approach this task, you can spin your wheels without gain. No one will hear your message. Be sure to tie your implementation ideas directly to your external social media goals.

External goals to consider include:

- Educate
- Inspire to action
- Create strong relationships
- Share internal culture with external audience
- Thought leadership
- Community involvement
- Sales
- Marketing
- Publicity

We elaborate on this task in the section *Create an External Social Computing Strategy* on page 82.

Create a Social Media Mission Statement

After reviewing your goals and strategy and creating drafts of your internal and social media strategies, create a mission statement for your social media efforts. This needs to be one sentence that everyone in your business can recite from memory. Doing so will help sharpen your thinking about your strategies and guide the creation of plans to support your social media goals.

Here are some examples of social media mission statements you can learn from.

> "Our mission is to drive forward the adoption of social media across Europe in order to improve the quality, access, value and effectiveness of healthcare delivery to patients."

> — Health Care and Social Media in Europe

This is an easy one to get started with. This non-profit exists to spread usage of social media. But notice that they directly tie this social media goal to a specific non-social-media goal: "to improve the quality, access, value and effectiveness of health-care delivery to patients." In other words, the organization doesn't just want to spread social media usage for its own sake; it wants to do so to achieve a real-world goal.

A great example of a very short and to-the-point mission statement is Ford's:

> "Humanize the Ford brand and put consumers in touch with Ford employees."

> — Scott Monty, Ford Motor Co.

You may have noticed that we don't even mention social media in the main title of our book, and this is intentional. The challenge for any business in the age of social media is to **Be a Person**, not a faceless entity. Scott Monty gets this. Ford wants to **Be a Person** — to humanize their brand, and connect with their community: their customers. So they put this in their social media mission statement. How can you get this concept into your statement?

Here's another statement that explicitly states what kind of person the business wants to be:

> "Instill trust in the brand, and highlight that the people behind the brand are parents too."

> — Lindsay Lebresco, Graco

Brilliant! Our employees are parents too; they can relate to you and your problems; they can create products that connect with your needs, because they share your needs. Wow.

Of course, delivering on your mission statement is the trick, isn't it?

Here's a general template to get you started on your social media mission statement:

> "The purpose of our social media efforts is to [*do something*] for [*someone*] while [*improving, furthering*] our [*business strategic objective*]."

Play with it until you think you've got it, and then get your staff involved in fine-tuning your statement.

Create Social Media Metrics

A strategy needs goals, and goals need measurement. Ensure that your social media goals can be measured. There's lots more about measurement in the section *Measure Results* in the full version of **Be a Person**, but for right now, you should think about real, concrete goals that are measurable.

We also talk much more about measuring the Return on Investment (ROI) of social media in the section *Measuring Social Media, Influence, Brand* in the full version of **Be a Person**, but here's a quick table of some of the things you can measure with social media:

Table 1 - Social Media Measurements

Blog posts	Google trends
Reader comments	Search results
Twitter mentions	Inbound traffic
Twitter followers	Video views
Facebook fans	SlideShare views
Links	Tags
RSS subscribers	Diggs

Don't worry too much if you don't understand what some of these elements are at this point. Most will become clear throughout the rest of the book.

Determine Who is Responsible

When creating your social media strategies, you should consider who in your business is going to be responsible for social media activities. We can't really do this for you, but here are some suggestions:

- Please don't just make it just marketing or public relations staff!

- Please don't make it just one person!

- How about anyone who touches clients?

- How about your leadership?

Determine How Your Clients Will Benefit

If you can't quantify this, you need to rethink your whole strategy. If the answer is truly that you see no benefit for external stakeholders, that's OK. Just be sure you understand that social media only provides internal benefits for your business. As we've discussed, those benefits can be enough.

Plan to Evolve Your Strategy

Accept that you're going to make mistakes. You're going to learn what works and what doesn't, and so you need to figure out how you are going to incorporate continuous improvement into your social media strategy and practice. One important element of improvement is to be open to innovation from your staff. Chances are good many have significant experience in social media and can help suggest improvements.

How is Social Media Relevant to Business?

First Steps Toward a Social Media Strategy

"Social Media Performance Group's motto is: **No Tools Before Rules**. We believe that before you use any powerful tool, you should not only find out its capabilities and dangers, but also create a plan for its use. Beginning to use social media without a strategy would be like tossing the keys of your SUV to your 10-year-old."

Social Media Performance Group

The Social Media Performance Group strategy process begins with an enterprise social media readiness assessment. You need to understand how ready your staff, leadership, board, and other stakeholders are to make the changes that will be necessary to embrace social computing.

Although you may not realize it at the planning stage, successfully implementing social media to support your strategies will require organizational changes, some large, some small, and some that may be upsetting or controversial. For example, if you're a business that has a strict command and control hierarchy where every external communication is approved at a high level, you'll need to change to be able to fully leverage social media. The legal department of one enterprise we know recently approved 40 tweets. Yeah, that'll work.

If the idea **Be a Person** scares you, you'll need to do some organizational transformation before social media is right for you.

Of course, not all businesses are ready for social computing. In fact there are some who have ingrained styles and tendencies that will make adopting social media impossible, if not actually detrimental. How can you tell if your business is one of them?

Top Ten Signs You Should Avoid Social Media

Lisa Barone, Chief Branding Officer of Outspoken Media, put together a somewhat humorous collection[37] of indicators of organizational dysfunction that would make adopting social computing a risky business. We've adapted and expanded them in the following list.

---

[37] Outspoken Media provides online marketing services. Barone's list is at: bit.ly/ctidjS

You have no social skills (and don't want to fake them)

If your organization has problems relating with staff, customers, or other stakeholders, those problems are likely to be magnified by using social computing. Be honest with yourself when assessing your organization's readiness to openly relate with a large group of your stakeholders.

You have no sense of humor/can't handle criticism

A sense of humor often doesn't make it onto the list of things to consider about social computing, but it should. If your organization gets stirred up by the least little bit of criticism, or has a habit of misinterpreting humorous comments, think twice before adopting social media. Using social media means you are opening yourself up to unvarnished dialog with both your supporters and your detractors. If you don't think you can handle it, social computing is not for you.

You're going to forget about it in the morning

Social computing takes a commitment. It can't be a start and stop kind of thing. Once you engage with your community, you aren't going to be able to go back to ignoring them. So be sure you have a long-term, sustainable commitment to social computing before venturing forth.

Openness is a problem for you

This one is pretty much self-explanatory. If your org-anizational style emphasizes secrecy, security, and a lack of sharing, you're not going to succeed with social computing. Ask yourself what you're hiding, and why, and whether you can open up before getting involved with social media.

You're only there to sell

If you think social computing is just about selling, or marketing, or pushing messages into just another media channel, better to forget it. Remember that social media involves relationships and two-way conversation, and that you must respect your comm-unity's point of view to be successful. You should also be wary if your leadership plans on having others masquerade as them online. Social media is about transparency, not facades.

You view social media as a numbers game

This is a common attitude toward social media. You see it on LinkedIn among the LIONs (There's more on that in the *What is a LinkedIn LION™?* section in the full version of **Be a Person**.) The number of followers on social media is generally not what your business should concentrate on. The quality of your interactions with your community is vastly more important than the quantity.

You sometimes resort to name calling

We decided to edit this one. Barone's original number 7 was: *You're inclined to call people's wives "douchettes."* Apparently, a CEO actually did call someone's wife a douchette,[38] although not online. Nevertheless, if your business has folks in it who might be inclined to disparage others, think twice about bringing this sort of thing to social computing.

You think Twitter is a social media strategy

We hope you know by now that we think you shouldn't get into social computing without first understanding how it can support your organization's strategy, and without creating a social media strategy to guide your usage. There are lots of consultants out there that think putting together a Twitter campaign, or a Facebook page, or a few YouTube videos is a great way to get started with social media. Tell that to Motrin.

You don't have a "social" culture

There are lots of signs of an anti-social-computing culture. The tendency to run everything by the lawyers. Endless rounds of revisions with final approval by top executives. A prohibition of social media site usage while at work. Blocking YouTube. Some of these tendencies can be overcome, and some

---

[38] Hear the audio at: **bit.ly/cymXi7**

might be enough to indicate problems with social computing acceptance. If your general organizational culture emphasizes tightly controlling the message, you're not likely to succeed with social media.

You don't have permission

In Barone's list, this item refers to staff who attempt to speak for the business without authorization, but we turn this around a little bit to mean, "Can you give your stakeholders permission to represent your business?" When you think about it, your staff, customers, and other stakeholders DO represent your business, every day, and can work on your behalf. But it's sometimes a hard step for an organization to let go enough to enable them to do the same on social media. Be sure you can let go before engaging with social media.

Do a Quick Survey of Your Stakeholders

To help determine if you're ready for social media, a social computing assessment can identify those who will embrace social computing, and who will resist. It also helps identify those who are willing but need training on how to use social computing.

The assessment can be done online using the Social Media Performance Group's free Social Media Readiness Survey™ [39] or via pen and paper using the version reproduced on page 55.

---

[39] SMPG's Social Media Readiness Survey: **bit.ly/smpgsurvey**

Do a Quick Survey of Your Customers

It is important to know what customers and prospects already know about social media so you can target your efforts to their ability to respond online. If your target audience is largely offline, you will want to use social media inside your company rather than externally.

It's important to realize that, due to socio-economic differences, many groups may not have regular access to social computing, which obviously can significantly alter your strategy in engaging them online. In your survey, you may want to segment prospects and customers by socio-economic status, which may affect how easily you can reach them via social media.

If your audience doesn't have computer-based online access, you may be able to reach them online via their mobile phones. In this case, you should consider using the Social Media Performance Group's free *Mobile Social Media Use Survey*.[40] The survey can also be found in the second part of the Social Media Performance Group Social Media Readiness Survey™, reproduced in the next section, and live at: **bit.ly/dBOx6X**

After your survey is done, take a look at the results and divide the respondents into at least two groups: those who are likely to respond to social media, and those who probably won't. You'll need to base your social media plans on the composition of these groups. If, for example, the non-social-media group represents the majority of your stakeholders, you may want to consider educational approaches to help them learn about the benefits of social media. On the other hand, if the social-media-using group is large, you may want to consider

---

[40] Social Media Performance Group's Mobile Social Media Use Survey: **bit.ly/c48q61**

more-sophisticated approaches to identify and enable your supporters via social media.

Assess Related Businesses

Identify closely-related businesses and partners you deal with on a regular basis, especially those with similar or complementary missions, particularly in your region. Find out what they are doing with social media. Not only might this give you ideas for your own approach, you may be able to team up with them to help further your social media reach.

Social Media Performance Group
Social Media Readiness Survey™

What is your comfort level with social networking/ media as of today?

___ I consider myself extremely proficient and knowledgeable in social networking/ media. I use it on a daily basis both professionally and personally.

___ I am comfortable with social networking/ media in a professional setting. I use social networking/ media frequently for business purposes.

___ I am comfortable with social networking/ media in a personally setting. I use social networking/ media frequently in my personal life.

___ I am familiar with social networking/ media but I am a casual user at best and I use it occasionally.

___ I know of social networking/ media but I don't use it at all.

___ I don't know anything about social networking/ media and as of right now, I am not comfortable with it and see no real value in it.

Please circle the appropriate answer as it applies to you.

I am very interested in learning more about social networking/ media, especially as it applies in a business setting.

Yes   No

I believe I would use social networking/ media more if I had a better understanding of it and how I could apply it in my professional life.

Yes   No

I believe that it is important to understand social networking/ media as it applies to business.

Yes   No

If I could see how other professionals are using social networking/ media in business I would be interested in learning more.

Yes   No

I believe social networking/ media is for personal use only and doesn't really apply to business.

Yes   No

I have no real interest in social networking/ media.

Yes   No

Social Networking/ Media Tools

How familiar are you with the following social media sites?

I'm a User	I Know of	None	Social Media Site
—	—	—	Linked In
—	—	—	Facebook
—	—	—	MySpace
—	—	—	You Tube (User: create content, Know Of: have used to watch videos)
—	—	—	Twitter
—	—	—	Blogging (I regularly read blogs or have my own blog)
—	—	—	Wikis (I regularly use wikis (such as Wikipedia) or have my own wiki)
—	—	—	Instant Messaging
—	—	—	Forums (I regularly participate in or have my own forum)
—	—	—	Ning
—	—	—	Business Social Networking Other (please list others) _____

—	—	—	Other personal social networking sites/ groups _____

Mobile Phones and Data Plans

Do you have a mobile phone?

Yes   No

Do you have a texting plan?

Yes   No

Do you have a smart phone with a data package?

Yes   No

How often do you do these activities on your mobile phone:

Daily	Weekly	Seldom	
—	—	—	Text
—	—	—	Email
—	—	—	Mobile Internet — Going to Websites

Daily	Weekly	Seldom	
___	___	___	Using Social Media

I sign up to be on email lists from companies

Yes   No

I sign up to receive text messages from companies

Yes   No

What kind of information do you find valuable and would want to receive via text message from companies?

Coupons   Sales   Special Events

Company Updates   For Social Purposes

I believe that mobile phones are very personal and I use mine for business because I have to.

Yes   No

I believe that mobile phones are personal and I don't want to receive anything on them other than phone calls from people I know.

Yes   No

Is Your Business Ready for Social Media?

There is a wide variety of skill sets required to be successful at social media, whether your business is just you and your computer or includes thousands of employees spread over several continents. Whether you're committing a couple hours a week, or you're hiring a social networking czar, your success will depend on the abilities of you and your team.

To find out if your business has the right stuff, consider giving your leadership and key stakeholders the following test, adapted and expanded from Ron Shulkin's blog.[41] Score one point for each "Yes" answer. Answer "Yes" if you or your team currently has the relevant ability or skill set.

On Your Marks

1. Are you passionate about social media and able to inspire your team and your community?

2. Are you willing to commit a significant percentage of your time to the social networking effort?

3. Can you objectively evaluate the readiness of your internal culture to adopt social media?

4. Can you establish marketing plans and a business social media strategy with clearly-identified, measurable goals?

------

[41] Ron Shulkin is Vice President for North America at CogniStreamer: bit.ly/dCfTWl

5. Can you articulate and sell-in a comprehensive social media strategy? (Comprehensive doesn't mean, "Let's try this and try that" rather how you'll use social media throughout your organization.)

6. Can you take responsibility for the success of your business's social media plan?

7. Can you marshal the organization's resources as required to execute the social media plan?

Get Set

8. Can you ensure daily updates to blogs and other social media that you are targeting by coordinating writing, publishing, promoting, and swift approvals?

9. Can you identify the software tools required to monitor your organization's social media activities and track progress toward measurable goals?

10. Do you have a reliable resource on staff that has a public relations or marketing degree or equivalent experience?

11. Can you find an excellent verbal and written communicator to be the public face of your effort?

12. Do you have experience with other successful online community building?

13. Do you have experience building and running a Website?

14. Are you well-versed in search engine optimization?

15. Do you have leadership and project management skills?

16. Do you have the stamina and patience to shepherd your business through the social media learning curve over a sustained period of time?

17. Do you have a strong familiarity with Facebook, LinkedIn, Twitter and YouTube?

18. Do you have in-depth knowledge of currently-available social media tools and the ability to use them to their best benefit?

19. Do you know what kinds of social media your target demographic uses most often?

Go

20. Do you stay current on the latest and best social media tools?

21. Can you provide guidance to your team members on social media best practices?

22. Can you define the rules of social media engagement for your business?

23. Do you have a plan to provide consistent messaging and brand promotion to those on your team who are engaging with your community?

---

24. Do you have relationships with industry-expert bloggers?

25. Do you have a plan and the means to develop videos, photographs, graphics, applications, and other digital multimedia presentations?

26. Are you a creative thinker who can develop interactive, intriguing and interesting ideas that can go viral?

27. Can you productively engage with detractors online rather than taking offense or responding emotionally?

Test Scoring:

26 — 27 points	You're ready! Get cracking!
23-25 points	You can start your planning
18-22 points	You're almost there, but will need to recruit some expertise
14-18 points	Plan on taking a few months developing your team and preparing your internal culture
13 or fewer points	Read this book. Twice. Be certain to ensure stakeholder buy-in because it will be six months or more before you're ready.

Decide What Your Business Will Do About Social Computing

"Not to decide is to decide."

Harvey Cox, American theologian

There's a huge opportunity out there for your business. Based on your organizational intentions and the assessments we've encouraged you to do, you have three choices:

- Ignore social media

- Monitor social media

- Engage with social media

Let's examine each of these choices in turn.

Ignore Social Media

Obviously, we think you shouldn't ignore social media, and a quick review of some of the risks of non-engagement should be sufficient to convince you that you must at least start to monitor social media.

Regulatory Risk

If your business has anything to do with securities or other types of regulation, you can't afford to ignore social computing. If you have large securities holdings, you may face restrictions on certain types of disclosures. If you aren't monitoring social media, you may not be aware of disclosures that involve your organization's staff and which may run afoul of regulations.

Your business may cite regulatory constraints as a reason to avoid getting involved in, or even monitoring, social media activities. Be sure that the risks of this approach don't outweigh your responsibility to ensure disclosures are proper.

Reputation Management

A related issue is reputation management. Your business may not have a formal reputation management effort, but every organization needs to be concerned with the subject. If you've ever subscribed to an article clipping service, you've been engaged in reputation management.

Social media is one of the largest and the fastest growing forums for people's opinions. You can't afford to ignore what people are saying about you online.

Ask these famous brands if ignoring social media was a good idea:

- Domino's disgusting video[42] in which a couple of immature employees with a video camera caused a huge crisis

- United breaks a guitar[43] and the customer gets even with a YouTube video

- Nestlé's Facebook Fan Page Heist[44] where people reacted to Nestlé's heavy-handed attempt to get a critical video removed from YouTube by posting altered versions of the firm's logo, culminating in a boycott

- KFC and Oprah's Free Chicken[45] — Winfrey announced that her show's Website would let visitors download a printable coupon for free Kentucky Grilled Chicken. Web servers were overloaded, and supplies of free chicken were exhausted. Bloggers reported that store managers were turning away coupon-holders. KFC chairman Roger Eaton posted a video message explaining that KFC would not be able to redeem the coupons still at large

There are lots more examples of dumb social media moves in our *Social Media Hall of Shame,* online at: **bit.ly/bjon3u**

---

[42] Domino's video: **rww.to/9LYuMs**

[43] United Breaks Guitars: **bit.ly/abJdu5**

[44] Nestlé Facebook Heist: **bit.ly/dzkXqb**

[45] KFC free chicken: **bit.ly/dan6ol**

Legal Issues of Disclosure

Chances are your business has some confidential information, whether it is client records or minutes of sensitive meetings or the like. We're sure you have policies that instruct staff and others on how to keep this information secure.

At the very least you need to update your policies to cover social computing. But you'll also probably want to monitor social media to detect any disclosures that do happen. In fact, it's even possible that failure to do so may leave you open to charges of negligence. Consult a lawyer for information about your responsibilities regarding social media disclosure.

Other Legal Issues

While everything in the following list from New York Employment Law Letter via HRHero.com[46] may not pertain to your enterprise, many items affect all businesses, profit or non-profit, large or small.

You can face potential liability from employee use of social networking sites or blogging in a variety of ways:

- **Slander, defamation, and libel** — Your company could be held liable if an employee posts negative statements about another person or a competitor on a Website or blog.
- **Trade secrets and intellectual property infringement** — The disclosure of certain trade secrets can destroy the "confidential" status of the information, and the disclosure of a third party's confidential information could lead to an

---

[46] bit.ly/9Xiop5

action for trade secret misappropriation or intellectual property infringement.

- **Trade libel** — Misstatements or misrepresentations about a competitor could lead to claims of trade libel.
- **Securities fraud and gun-jumping** — Publicly traded companies can face sanctions for securities fraud if material misrepresentations are posted. Any postings plugging the registered company could violate federal securities law.
- **Employment actions** — Employees may try to sue you for wrongful termination or discrimination if their employment is terminated because of postings that reference personal aspects of their life (*for example,* marital status or sexual orientation).
- **Harassment** — Language that is harassing, discriminatory, threatening, or derogatory could prompt a lawsuit.

As always, you should seek legal counsel only from a lawyer and not from a book such as this or the Web.

Your Community Might Expect Social Media Responses

As the social computing movement gains momentum, it is becoming more and more common that stakeholders expect a response to complaints or other comments made online. Depending on your business, you may not be in this position today, but you will probably be in the near future.

This is especially true if you've dipped your social media toe in the water and have a Twitter or Facebook account that you don't monitor. Being on social media sets up an expectation that you will monitor and respond. As we've said before, don't get involved until you're ready to make a commitment for the long term.

Thinking Social Computing is Irrelevant

Despite our enthusiasm, and the probable enthusiasm of some of the people around you, you need to take all this social media stuff with a grain of salt.

At the present moment, it's very possible that what works online may work just fine offline as well. The two environments, while they do track closely on many fronts, are not identical.

The big brands have taken notice of this fact. In a 2009 article[47] in Advertising Age, Abbey Klaassen talks about the difference between what the general population is interested in versus what Twitter users are interested in:

> For example, in the past month [April, 2009], the Twitter community has been titillated by South by Southwest, AT&T, "Lost" and the redesign of Skittles.com. Missing from the list are things [that] the Communispace and Lightspeed surveys, both separately commissioned on Ad Age's behalf, found that the general population is fired up about, such as the AIG bonuses and the bank-bailout plans.

So offline does not equal online, yet.

Given the risks, however, social media shouldn't be ignored. But it also shouldn't be treated as the be-all and end-all for your organization. And as time goes on, the growth of social media will continue, and the two worlds will track much more closely. So if you do choose to ignore social media for now, don't do so for too long.

---

[47] Using Social Media to Listen to Consumers: **bit.ly/bGFtdl**

Monitor Social Media

If you decide that you aren't ready to engage with social computing but you can't afford to ignore it, a low-risk option is to merely monitor what is being said about your enterprise online.

There are lots of free and paid options for monitoring social media and some of them are quite complex, allowing for the semi-automated determination of a concept called sentiment.

Sentiment generally measures how people who are talking about you online feel about you. Social monitoring tools can recognize angry, sad, positive, happy, and a variety of other sentiments by extracting terms from online text.

Monitoring of message texts and sentiment is a key component to measuring the effect of your social media efforts, and it can also help you get acclimated to listening to your community. We talk about this in greater detail in the sections *Listen to Your Community* and *Measure Results* in the full version of **Be a Person**.

We recommend that you start monitoring social media well in advance of any initial attempts to use it. Once you start listening, you may be surprised at what people are saying, both negative and positive.

One of the great things about social computing is you can potentially see everything people are saying about you online. One of the sobering things is you might not like what you see.

If you're an organization of any size, you've had people bad-mouthing you for your entire existence. No business is perfect, and there are lots of people who do nothing but find fault. Before there was online, people were talking negatively about you, but you couldn't always hear.

With social media, not only you can hear the bad things people are saying, you can respond and engage with the speakers.

Isn't that great? We think that's fantastic! For the first time in history, you have the opportunity to engage with your detractors, and perhaps change their minds or mitigate their effect. See a good example of how doing so can turn a negative into a positive in the section *Engage and Clarify* in the full version of **Be a Person**. Being able to answer your critics is an unprecedented advantage for your enterprise, and how you deal with it will be important for your success with social media.

We strongly recommend that if you cannot productively engage with naysayers, you should ignore them. If you engage with them in a non-productive way (denying their validity, calling them names), you can do way more harm than good.

If you're just in monitoring mode, of course, you won't start engaging; you'll just be listening to what people say about you. You may be tempted to engage, but we recommend that you wait until you've listened for a while, and until you've got a plan for how to approach both the supporters and the detractors. Get your social computing strategy together first before engaging. It's too risky to do otherwise.

What if you are listening and no one is talking about your business? How do you get them to start talking? Well, first you start by engaging with social media.

Engage with Social Media

Obviously, we think you should engage with social media, but only if your organizational assessment determines that you can make it a positive experience both for the enterprise and your stakeholders.

Josh Mendelsohn, Vice President of Chadwick Martin Bailey sums it up nicely:

> While social media is not the silver bullet that some pundits claim it to be, it is an extremely important and relatively low cost touch point that has a direct impact on sales and positive word of mouth.
>
> Companies not actively engaging are missing a huge opportunity and are saying something to consumers — intentionally or unintentionally — about how willing they are to engage on consumers' terms.[48]

Mendelsohn's company surveyed 1,500 consumers and found those who are Facebook fans and Twitter followers of a brand are more likely to not only recommend, but also more likely to buy from those brands than they were before becoming fans/ followers.

So there are some pretty compelling reasons to get engaged.

If you've been through the assessments and caveats we've presented above, and you think you're ready, then begin with an examination of your current organizational strategy, and fit your social computing strategy to it. The next section can help guide you in this process. After you have created your social computing strategies, see the section *How to Engage with Social Computing* on page 109.

---

[48] Chadwick Martin Bailey is custom market research and consulting firm: **bit.ly/izHMWz**

Create Social Computing Strategies

"Over and over again, connecting people
with one another is what lasts online.
Some folks thought it was about
technology,
but it's not. "

Seth Godin, interactive marketing expert

Let's say you want to remodel your kitchen. A contractor visits and begins to describe his approach: "I'm going to use a screwdriver and some screws; a hammer and some nails; a saw and some wood; a sledgehammer and a crowbar."

Another contractor visits and shows you the plans for the new kitchen, a list of materials you'll have to buy, and a project plan with a timeline and a cost.

Which contractor would you trust your kitchen project with?

It's the same with social media. You may encounter social media consultants who talk about LinkedIn, and Facebook, and Twitter, and YouTube, and Flickr, and Digg, and blogs and on and on. They may express great enthusiasm about the latest cool tools, and may encourage you to just try social media — do a quick project and just see what happens.

Hey, kids! Let's set up a Twitter account! Just as with the kitchen renovation, you're better off having a strategy, a plan, and a design before you consider the tools you'll use to engage your community via social media.

Social Media Performance Group's motto, "No Tools Before Rules™" means take the time to first determine what social media can do to support the strategy and goals of your enterprise. Then create a social media strategy, and map it to all the areas of your organization, inside and out. Only then should you begin to talk about tactics and tools. Your brother-in-law's 20-year-old nephew might seem like a good option to help you get started, but he's not likely to have the depth of understanding of your strategy, and of social media strategy, to ensure that you won't just waste your time and money on an ineffective Facebook fan page, for example.

With social media, like a lot of things on the Web, you can't build it and expect them to come.

So how do you get started? First, think about the makeup of a good social computing strategy.

Elements of a Social Computing Strategy

As we've said, your social computing strategy should map social computing activities to your enterprise's overall goals and objectives. In addition, a good social computing strategy:

- Effectively communicates goals and benefits of social media internally and externally
- Guides selection of the right tools to use
- Ensures sustainability of your social media endeavor
- Involves regular reviews of people, processes, and tools to ensure that your business stays relevant

Specifically, a social computing strategy addresses how your enterprise will:

- Approach social media
  - Create the messaging
  - Handle community responses, positive and negative
  - Create and maintain social computing policy
  - Maintain the connection between organizational strategy and social computing strategy
- Join the conversation
  - Determine how to **Be a Person**, not an organization — who gets to speak online?
  - Determine how to listen
  - Find community members
  - Engage your community
    - Ask for their help
    - Who manages your community?
  - Measure your social computing success
- Ensure safe social computing
  - Manage legal issues

- o Manage your online reputation
- Brand your business online
  - o Determine how your main Website supports your social computing initiatives
  - o Determine kinds of online branding campaigns to focus on
  - o Manage the connection between online and offline branding
- Find and create online evangelists
  - o Determine the kinds of people to cultivate as evangelists
  - o Support evangelist development and sustain existing evangelists
- Create buzz
  - o Examine types of online and offline promotions
  - o Manage and sustain online buzz
- Attract and convert new customers, staff, and evangelists
  - o Create online rules of engagement
  - o Prioritize outreach techniques
- Encourage and manage eCommerce
  - o Plan prospect conversion
  - o Foster recommendations, ratings, and research
  - o Coordinate with offline techniques

You can use this list as an outline as you create your organization's overall social computing strategy. We elaborate on many of these points in later sections of this book and the rest in the full version of **Be a Person**.

Create an Internal Social Computing Strategy

Many people think of social computing as an externally-oriented thing. The popularity of the various large social media sites — Facebook, LinkedIn, Twitter, YouTube — encourages enterprises to think social media is only about external relationships.

In reality, one of the more powerful ways to use social computing is inside your organization. In fact, as we've said, we believe that sales and marketing may be the least impressive things that social computing does. Social media can help build a sense of community among your employees, help improve internal communications, and greatly increase staff retention.

As we've mentioned, beginning by following an internal social computing strategy may be a lower-risk way to get started with social media. Whether this is your attitude or not, you should definitely create an internal social computing strategy. This strategy should support your enterprise's overall strategy and your external social computing strategy. And if the community you address has challenges in getting computer-based access to social media, you should also create a mobile social computing strategy.

Create your internal social computing strategy to help:

- Communicate with your base
- Energize your base
- Help your base communicate your enterprise's goals and objectives
- Create evangelists

Your internal social computing strategy should communicate to all stakeholders:

- What the business is
- How each stakeholder supports the mission — and each other
- How to use internal social media
- Policies
- How-to's
- Their responsibility in creating internal and external community

Your internal social computing strategy should:

- Leverage your assessment of staff's strengths and weaknesses so you can assign tasks accordingly
- Create an internal communication system to quickly and easily communicate social media strategy, tactics, and techniques
- Ensure that employees create profiles within chosen social media tools and actively use them
- Identify one or two people to be in charge of social media (both internal and external)
- Ensure your enterprise keeps a unified voice to the outside

Some of the organizational pain points you might want to address with your internal strategy include:

- **Inefficient Communications** — Communicating among staff or between staff and partners may rely entirely on email. This can often be inefficient as large files get emailed or recipients forget where or if they have them, resulting in redundancy and inefficiency. Consider how using social computing techniques such as internal blogs or wikis could help.

- **Ineffective Collaboration** — If your staff must collaborate on projects by, say, jointly revising a document, the back and forth of changes, and the difficulty in collecting and applying them can be challenging. In addition, reporting status via email may be prone to confusion if everyone doesn't follow the email thread. Using social computing features such as document repositories and project-based collaborative blogging may help.
- **Rampant Rumor Mongering** — One way to know if your organization seems disconnected from its leadership is the quantity of rumors that circulate within it. A leadership blog can help establish a connection between management and staff. Enabling comments on the blog can help leaders get a pulse on staff attitudes as well as foster innovation.

These are just a few ideas on ways social computing can help your enterprise. When crafting your internal strategy, look for these and other ways you can foster the social cohesion and communication of your company using social computing.

For example, as we've mentioned, using social media internally can greatly increase staff satisfaction at a relatively low cost.[49] Using forums and Twitter direct messaging can help your teams communicate better and in real-time. Using a wiki can help you capture the organizational knowledge that often walks out the door when an employee quits.

---

[49] Just one example of the many articles and studies that support this: SocialTimes' *How to Connect With Your Employees Using Social Media, Email and Some Common Sense* **bit.ly/9o1vnP**

Create an External Social Computing Strategy

Create an external strategy to:

- Communicate with prospects and customers
- Recruit new evangelists and influencers
- Create a network of partners to multiply the effect of your own sales and marketing efforts

It is becoming well-accepted that today's social-media-savvy users do not respond as readily as they once did to pushed marketing messages (TV, radio, newspapers, magazine advertising).[50] Social media transforms an old sales platitude — "People do not like to be sold, but they love to buy" — into "People love buying from their friends. Make someone your friend and they will buy from you."

The advertising industry knows this, according to the Chief Creative Officer of the world's 4th largest ad agency, Craig Davis of J. Walter Thompson:

> Audiences everywhere are tough. They don't have time to be bored or brow-beaten by orthodox, old-fashioned advertising. We need to stop interrupting what people are interested in & **be** what people are interested in.[51]

So it's likely that your average prospect is barraged daily with appeals and pitches, which they can become quite adept at ignoring. Social media, on the other hand, creates value by fostering a relationship with an organization and a brand, rather

---

[50] Fournaise Marketing Group, **bit.ly/bAkvPe** bit.ly/dmwcg9

[51] Exist.com: **bit.ly/kj6p4l**

---

than creating another loud member of a clamoring crowd.

A social computing strategy has become a must, particularly for large enterprises, and incorporating social media into an organization's overall strategy ensures that social media becomes an integrated driver of relationships, brand loyalty, and sales, rather than a less-effective afterthought.

Social Media Performance Group Approach

Our approach to creating a social computing strategic plan is designed to first and foremost integrate with your organization's strategic goals. We believe attacking a point opportunity ("Let's do some tweets about our new product") or a tactical implementation ("Let's drive traffic to our YouTube client testimonials") without alignment with your enterprise's strategy not only misses much of the value social media can bring to an organization, but also risks becoming counterproductive.

In addition, if all social media efforts are not coordinated with clear objectives and metrics, your organization runs the risk of wasting money and effort and losing effectiveness.

We lay out the elements of a successful approach to a social computing strategy in the sections that follow.

Review Business Strategy

As a first step, as we've indicated in previous sections, conduct a review of your enterprise's strategy, goals, and implementation plans to ensure alignment of the social media strategy. Next, work with your organization's senior leaders to create an enterprise-wide strategic blueprint. Determine how social media will support your operations, employees, sales, service delivery, and so on.

During this process, you should examine all the potential social media touch points for your enterprise, both internally and externally. We suggest you look beyond the usual suspects when thinking about how social media can help your company.

Who are the usual suspects? Typically, the leading purveyors of social media solutions in businesses of all sizes are public relations and marketing, and it's likely the same for your organization. The *2009 Digital Readiness Report*,[52] found that PR and Marketing lead the vast majority of social media engagements inside businesses of all types and sizes:

- In 51 percent of businesses, PR leads digital communications compared to 40.5 percent where marketing leads
- PR is responsible for blogging at 49 percent of all businesses vs. marketing's 22 percent
- PR is responsible for micro-blogging (think Twitter) at 52 percent of all businesses vs. 22 percent for marketing, for a combined 74 percent

We think this state of affairs misses the point of social media, which, for us, is about relationships between people, not pushing PR and marketing messages. And the cool thing is you've got people all over your organization who can create relationships. By letting the PR and marketing folks in your enterprise dominate your social media use, you'll miss lots of places where social media can contribute to your organization.

When we help enterprises realize the value of social media, we

---

[52] Produced by iPressroom, a hosted content management software platform, with support from the Public Relations Society of America: **bit.ly/djp0cw**

---

do this based on our proprietary Enterprise Social Media Framework™ (ESMF). The ESMF maps your organization's structure to social media best practices and includes dozens of illustrative case studies pulled from the experiences of non-profit and for-profit organizations from all over the world.

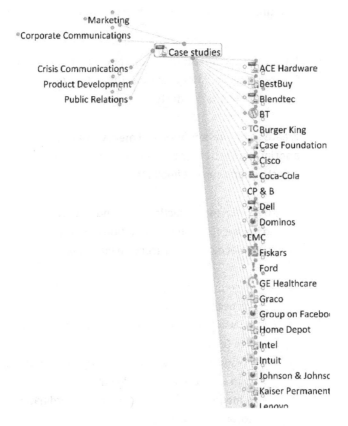

Figure 4- A small section of the Case Study area of ESMF

You can contact us if you're interested in learning more about ESMF. Otherwise, take a look at what has been successful for enterprises like yours and think about how the advantages of social media can help you beyond PR and marketing.

Finally, decide which opportunities to address first, and develop implementation plans.

Comprehensive Strategic Approach

We propose that you take a comprehensive approach in which you:

- **Analyze the competition** — Everyone has competition. Ensure that your enterprise is positioned to succeed against competitors' efforts

- **Create a comprehensive social media strategy** — Develop a social media strategy that is intimately bound to your objectives and current implementations

- **Create a social media tactical plan and structure** — Be sure to iterate out all implementation details to create a turnkey social media infrastructure including:

  - A community space on your organization's Website where users can comment
  - A facility to capture client reviews, suggestions, and testimonials
  - Presence on all relevant social media sites along with tactical plans for using them
  - A model for involving partners in coordinating social media campaigns
  - Social media monitoring services

- **Ensure social media training for your enterprise** — You'll need to assess and train your organization as well as designating community manager(s) and others who will implement your tactics. If you're interested, you can outsource ongoing community management and other social media execution to Social Media Performance Group, or we can train your staff to fulfill these functions.

Integrate Search with the Social Media Strategy

Social media must be integrated with Search Engine Marketing (SEM) and Search Engine Optimization (SEO) efforts. Your enterprise may not be involved with such efforts at this point. That may be a mistake. SEM and SEO are critical to the success of any Web site these days.

With recent moves by Google to index Facebook and Twitter, social media's influence on online search is accelerating to the point that leading-edge firms are increasingly talking about a new term, Social Search Optimization (SSO). [53] We talk about social search in the section *Real-Time Social Search* in the full version of **Be a Person**.

All your Web sites should follow good Search Engine Optimization processes, so you should review current practices and determine how social media interacts with SEO. (We cover this in the *Find Your Community* section in the full version of **Be a Person**.) Among the areas that you should address are page content, titles and metadata, content positioning, underlying codebase, site navigation, sitemap, and URL structure.

Create and implement a Social Search Optimization strategy, including identifying keywords and analyzing competitive sites. See the sections *Advanced Google Searching* and *Optimizing*

---

[53] Some Social Search Optimization resources: **slidesha.re/dTdBDM** **slidesha.re/dQ68z3** slidesha.re/igunmG

for Google in the full version of **Be a Person** for more information on using Google and SEO.

Writing Your Social Media Strategy

Work with your organization to identify and implement your organization-wide social media strategy and associated implementation plans. The following are the main social media areas that will require development and implementation.

Determine Important Points

Develop a set of talking points that will be used to engage potential evangelists and supporters using social media. The points may change over time, as you learn more about your community.

The talking points should emphasize the special qualities of your business's services and foster a personal relationship with your brand. They should sound natural if delivered by an average person and should appeal to the emotional connection that your best customers feel with your enterprise's products or services. However, the message needs to be customized by audience as much as possible, so you may need to develop several groups of talking points.

Identify Influencers

All people using social media are not equal in their ability to influence others. Identify those who are already talking about and recommending your products or services, especially those with a significant online and social media presence. You may, for example, start with your organization's customer support people and concentrate on those who actively work with your clients.

Create talking points for these influencers and think of other ways to enable them to help spread the word. The message will spread better if it is more easily found, and influencers can help your business's messages and products place higher in search engine results as well.

The goal is to quickly develop a number of evangelists, those who feel passionate about your products and your business and who will, with a little support, happily pass on information and help to convert others.

Create a Brand for the Social Media Effort

A good online movement needs a name. The name should be short, catchy, and communicate the goals of the effort. Building on the research efforts above, create the name and then use it to brand all campaign efforts. Your organization's site and partner Websites must help support the branding, and prominently feature selected user-generated content (UGC) in support of the campaign.

A great example of this was Yum! Brands' *Crash the Super Bowl* campaign[54] which encouraged people to submit ideas for Doritos commercials to run during Super Bowl XLV. Some of the user-generated ads were celebrated as the best presented during the entire broadcast.

Now this was a glitzy, highly costly campaign — especially considering the $1 million price tag for an advertising slot. But your enterprise might do a similar campaign, for far less money, to encourage your supporters to offer you ideas for your YouTube channel. This type of approach is called crowdsourcing, and we talk about it in the full version of **Be a Person**.

---

[54] Crash the Superbowl: **bit.ly/hAIYId**

Establish a More-Effective and Coordinated Social Media Presence

The best way to get into social media is to start to participate (after creating a strategy and first listening for a while, of course!)

The best way to participate is to engage people one-on-one through active listening, rather than pushing advertising messages at them.

This strategy involves building on any existing enterprise social media assets such as customer stories and testimonials, YouTube videos, Twitter accounts and other sites. Create presences on popular social networking sites as well as engaging with those who are already using social media to discuss your products and your business.

All these efforts should be coordinated, and revolve around the talking points. Consider creating a branded social networking site that enables user-generated content, either standalone or as part of your organization's site. You should recognize, however, that this is a substantial undertaking. We talk about architecting your own community in the section *Building Your Community* in the full **Be a Person** book.

Capitalize on Existing Relationships

Ensure that all stakeholders whom the enterprise touches regularly — your organization's sales and marketing folks as well as customer service and product management — are kept up-to-date via social media and other means.

This means leveraging any existing Internet assets such as email lists as well as other established marketing and public relations partners and also encouraging stakeholders to reach out to those they can influence.

Leverage Traditional Media Resources

Fold the social media campaign in with traditional marketing efforts such as press releases and other media contacts. Ensure that the campaign's brand is extended into traditional media. And remember: Don't stop doing anything you're already doing just because you're now doing social media. Ensure that all your efforts reinforce one another.

Enable Direct Supporter Actions

Provide media assets such as videos, screensavers, and special badges[55] to evangelists and other supporters. This concept extends to all forms of user-generated content, including blogs/posts, audio, and especially email.

Create a Mobile Social Computing Strategy

Many of your prospects may not have regular access to computers or the Internet, and others may prefer mobile devices for their daily social media use. You may want to create a non-Web-based social computing strategy to leverage:

- Smart mobile phones
- Tablets such as iPads and Android pads
- Texting

Mobile social computing is becoming a very important way users are interacting with social media. According to Facebook, in February, 2010 more than 100 million people were using Facebook from their mobile devices every month. That represents a growth of 53 percent in just six months, as

---

[55] See the definition of badges on page 19

there were just 65 million[56] users of using Facebook Mobile[57] in September 2009.

In fact, a recent study[58] by Ground Truth found that US mobile users spend almost 60 percent of their time on social networks.

Percent of Time Spent on Mobile Internet Usage by Category

Category	Percent
Social Networking	59.83%
Portals	13.65%
Operator	9.02%
Messaging	7.35%
Mobile Downloads	1.27%
All Other	8.88%

MySpace and Facebook were the top destinations cited in the study, which brings up an interesting point: Mobile users may not be the same demographic as computer-based social media users. Facebook has many times the number of members as the fading MySpace, yet MySpace was the most popular destination for mobile users, followed closely by Facebook. No other highly-popular social media sites were in the top 10 in the study.

---

[56] Source: Facebook **bit.ly/9fE4qn**

[57] Facebook Mobile. on.fb.me/bpiCmQ

[58] Ground Truth is a mobile computing research firm: **bit.ly/caaE65**

MySpace's demographic skews young, with a generally higher proportion of high-school-age and younger users.

So if you want to reach mobile users, you'll need to adjust your approach and your messaging.

There is even research that indicates that mobile social media use is more popular than computer-based usage. A study by Ruder Finn in February, 2010[59] found:

- 91 percent of mobile phone users go online to socialize compared to only 79 percent of traditional desktop users

- Mobile phone users are 1.6 times more likely to bank online compared to traditional desktop users (62 percent versus 39 percent)

Based on these statistics, you may find that you need to create a mobile social computing strategy that is slightly different from the rest of your external strategy. Since many social media sites are not optimized for the restricted bandwidth and small screen size of mobile phones, you may want to concentrate your efforts on sites that better-support these devices. Facebook has been a leader in this area.

---

[59] Ruder Finn is a public relations firm: **bit.ly/djlLb8**

Where to Go from Here

There's much more on these social computing strategy components in the full version of **Be a Person**, along with a lot of how-to advice.

But for now, let's take a look at some overall rules for using social computing, in the next section.

The 10 Commandments of Social Computing

"I think our nature is to be active and engaged. I've never seen a 2-year-old or a 4-year-old who's not active and engaged. That's how we are out of the box. And if you begin with this presumption, you create much more open, flexible arrangements that almost inevitably lead to greater satisfaction for individuals and great innovation for organizations."

Daniel Pink, media theorist

Social Networking, Social Media, Social Computing — whatever you call it, it's big, it's new, and it's growing rapidly.

We've collected several rules for using social media as the 10 Commandments of Social Computing.[60]

Thou shall not social network for the sake of social networking

Social Media is Not:	Social Media is:
A Fad	Relevant to the Enterprise
Just For Kids	For Everyone
About New Channels to Push Messages	About Creating Conversations
About the Tools	About Strategy
About the Techniques	About Planning and Execution
A Numbers Game	About Creating Relationships
A Replacement	A Supplement to Existing Techniques

---

[60] For other folks' 10 commandments, see:
bit.ly/c2L97N
bit.ly/9NWATb
bit.ly/c5s IZT
bit.ly/ceUjEs
and bit.ly/8ZNxQG

Thou shall not abuse social networking

Quick Tips

- Don't push, push, push
- It's a conversation, not a soapbox!
- Avoid over-updating
    - Example: being 1 of 200 friends on Facebook, but making up 25 percent of updates — You're not that important!
    - Don't send out multiple requests to join your social media group or fan your page — If they want to join, THEY WILL!
- Avoid too many email blasts

Don't Push, Push, Push

People who do marketing are used to pushing their message out indiscriminately, hoping to somehow connect with those who will respond. In the traditional marketing environment, there is little way to identify ready recipients of the message, and marketers spend billions each year trying to segment the market and deliver the right message to the right person.

Social Media is different in three important ways:

- You can have conversations with prospects
- You can know more about your prospects and understand better how they will respond
- You can actually more-directly measure the effect of your efforts to attract and inform them

---

Because the medium offers these advantages, social computing users do not respond as well to the traditional push style of marketing. They may even be insulted if you blindly push your message at them.

Increasingly, online users respond better to relationship marketing.

It's a conversation, not a soapbox!

Avoid Over-Updating

If you're constantly updating your status, posting to your blog or otherwise creating a high volume of messages in your social media venues, fellow users are likely to see you as annoying.

For example, if you post a high volume of Facebook status updates, your friends may either tune you out or hide your updates.

It's not all about you. It's about the relationships and community that you build.

Similarly, if your messaging is one-note — join my mailing list, buy my product, recommend my product — people will stop listening. You must balance your overt messaging with other messages of interest, either on or off topic. You'll need to discover the exact proportions that work for your community for yourself, but a good rule of thumb is to contribute four times for every time you ask for something.

Imagine you're at a cocktail party. You are making the rounds and you start to talk to someone who, although he's talking about a topic you're interested in, totally dominates the conversation and constantly asks you to come to his seminar and learn more.

Do you hang out with this person, or do you find an excuse to move on, and never re-engage with him?

Social media is like a big cocktail party. The boring monologists often end up speaking only to themselves.

How do you know if you're over-sharing? Ask. Often. But not too often! 【ツ】

Thou shall focus on connections and community

People join social networks to be a part of something bigger than themselves. So it follows that most of the time, that something bigger is not you (personally) or even your product or service. Remember, no matter how successful your community or your Website is, people will spend 99 percent of their online time elsewhere. So be careful to give them what they expect, and what they want, while they're at your place.

One of the main things people want online is for their voices to be heard, especially by others who are passionate about a product, issue, or topic. Enable that. Support their desire to be heard, to be valued, and to connect. What you say is important; what they say is essential.

Everyone is looking for a group that accepts them for who they are. Your job in creating a social media space is to foster that acceptance by giving them the tools, the space, and the permission to become a cohesive, self-sustaining group. That's the Holy Grail.

People want relationships that translate into the real world, not just online! Nobody spends all their time online (well, they've at least got to answer the door and pay the pizza guy). Many people look to make their online time and relationships meaningful in TRW (The Real World). There are many ways you can encourage these offline connections:

- Have real-world meetups[61] where virtual friends can press the flesh
- Show your followers evidence of how your customers love your products or services by providing testimonials — written and via video or audio — from satisfied and enthusiastic customers
- Encourage your followers to share details from their own lives, and how your business has helped them

Thou shall not commit social networking narcissism

Narcissus was so in love with his image that he gazed at it all day, to the exclusion of other activities. Sound like anyone you know online?

The Web is full of people who are full of themselves — the kind who might say, "Enough about me. What do you think about me?" Many enterprises act the same way online, showing an alarming sense of self-absorption. They may be talking with you, but conversation is one way — all about them, their business, their marketing program, their issues and obstacles, their successes.

One sign of social networking narcissism may be, as we've previously mentioned, constantly updating your status on Facebook, Twitter, LinkedIn, or other social sites. This is like push advertising and your contacts will soon tire of hearing all about you, especially if your status is boring trivia such as,

---

[61] Meetup.com allows people to organize real-world networking meetings online: **bit.ly/btNB8n**

"The line at Starbucks is long" or "My cat just rolled over" or "Going up the stairs." Yes, these are all real tweets!

Of course, you may be over-sharing about your enterprise as well. Remember, it's not all about you, your group, your business! You need to be interesting first, and interested always. This means you comment on other people's posts; you send them messages asking how they're doing; you help develop and sustain a relationship with your contacts.

Narcissism, self-promotion, and boring/excessive status updates are often cited as the top reasons people "unfriend" or disconnect with others online.[62]

Finally, the form of your communication also counts. Don't just make statements; ask questions, and especially open-ended questions, even if they're off-topic: What's your favorite movie? What's your best idea for promoting our products? What could we be doing better?

Thou shall balance business and pleasure in social networking

Social networking is supposed to be fun; don't make it all business. Don't be ultra-serious all the time. Sure, your business is serious, and important, but acknowledge that there are other sides to life, and don't be afraid to have fun. Make a stupid pun. Link to the latest stupid LOLCat picture (**bit.ly/dspJnq**) or dumb YouTube video (**bit.ly/9SQgex**). It's all about adding value, and sometimes that value is bringing a smile to your contacts' faces.

---

[62] Reasons to unfriend: **bit.ly/asCl5j**

Remember, you are competing with all sorts of entertainment, online and offline. You may find that a light and humorous tone may attract more followers or deepen existing relationships.

Be a Person! Be personal. Share things about yourself. Ask others for their opinions.

The more real you are, the better the online and offline relationship!

Thou shall be relevant

It's not about your agenda — Talk about what's important to your audience.

Sure you want to make your points about your products or services, but do so in relation to your audience's needs and interests.

One of the keys to social media success is providing what they want, not necessarily pushing what you want. Be relevant to their lives, even if it means straying off point. You want a relationship, a true, two-way understanding with your community. Think of the significant relationships in your life. How many of them are one-dimensional, built only upon a common interest in bowling, music, fishing, novels, disaster movies, or whatever?

Chances are in your best, most significant personal relationships, you connect on many levels. Ensure that you do that via social media as well.

Thou shall customize your strategy for your target groups

Before you even start using social media to improve your relationship to your followers, be sure you know who they are, how they differ, and how they want to be addressed.

How can you find these things out? Ask them.

Take the example of Fiskars, the Finnish manufacturer you probably know, if you know of them at all, as a maker of scissors. Scissors. A pretty boring category. Who cares what brand of scissors you buy? How utterly, utterly dull.

Well, if that's the way you feel, you couldn't be more wrong.

Think about Fiskars' audience. What are they doing with the scissors (and punches, shape cutters, stampers, craft trimmers, embossers, knives and multitools, edgers, and other craft tools)?

They're scrapbooking and doing other crafts.

If you know any scrapbookers, you know they can be very passionate, even fanatical. And they are inherently social. They like to get together IRL (In Real Life) and swap ideas, and work on their projects together.

So Fiskars did a very smart thing, way back in 2006: They created the Fiskateers social media site.[63]

How did they start their site? They found four women who were committed to scrapbooking and made them the heads of

---

[63] Fiskateers site: **bit.ly/9oBR3R**

a nationwide campaign to create online and offline places (retail stores) for people bound by this common interest to gather and share ideas and community.

The site won awards. It generated results:

- 6,250 members in 50 states
- 1,000 certified volunteer demonstrators
- In craft stores where Fiskateers are involved Fiskars has three-times-higher sales growth than in non-member stores
- 13 new product ideas/month
- 85 percent of "Fiskateers" are likely to recommend the product to a friend[64]

And, by the way, Fiskars spent less than $500,000 on this effort.

So you need to understand the segments of your target market. And you need a strategy for dealing with each. For sure there are some you will not be able to reach online. But a surprising number will not only respond to you online, they're already there and talking about you and your enterprise. Find their communities, listen, and tailor your approach to their needs.

So your question is: Can you find four women? (Or eight men. 【ツ】)

---

[64] Adam Singer, blogging about Jackie Huba's (Church Of The Customer) Keynote at MIMA Summit Oct 5th, 2009: **bit.ly/cPol5P**

Thou shall balance online activities with real world activities

For best results, social networking relationships should translate into real world action of some kind. This action may be face-to-face (F2F) meetings, commitments to act to publicize or endorse your products, or some other action such as sales.

Social networking is a way to stay connected in between real world events. If your enterprise has periodic events, social networking can keep participants connected and top-of-mind in the intervals between real world community meetings.

Social networking is a dynamic way to quickly get the word out about real world events. Combine it with your normal online promotions, such as email lists, newsletters and online advertising.

If you put all your eggs in the social networking basket, you may one day realize that you've lost some of the real world connections you built up over the years.

Thou shall not try to control everything

As we've discussed, social media is about the community, not about you. And that implies that you have to give up some control in order to do social media. You may be used to thinking you're in control of your brand, your message. Well, you never really were. What people think about you has always been your brand.

Leroy Stick, the anonymous person behind the satirical, faux BP Twitter account, @BPGlobalPR, perhaps said it best: "So what is the point of all this? The point is, FORGET YOUR BRAND. You don't own it because it is literally nothing. You can spend all sorts of time and money trying to manufacture public opinion, but ultimately, that's up to the public, now isn't it?"[65]

People have always talked about you (if you're lucky), and sometimes they say bad things about you. Now their talk is visible on the social Web, and you can see, perhaps too vividly, what your brand is, and what messages your community produces about — you!

To engage the community, you're going to need to give up control.

You won't control the conversation. You won't control the venue (close your site and they'll go elsewhere and bad-mouth you). You won't control how people react to you.

Giving up control is the toughest thing for all businesses — You're not alone!

Social networking is dynamic; it belongs to the participants; it's not about control, it's about empowering people and energizing them to act on your behalf.

Social networking is about relationships, and relationships are based on a level of trust, not control.

But what if people are saying bad things about me, you ask.

Face it, if you act in the world, you'll always have detractors. The difference social media brings is that now you can not only see what people are saying about you, you can react, in real time, and, by engaging them, perhaps change their minds.

This capability alone is worth giving up some control, isn't it?

---

[65] Leroy Stick's blog post on StreetGiant: **bit.ly/btswHj**

Thou shall enable people to become online evangelists

Not only can you find the naysayers online, you can also find your supporters.

Your goal should be to identify, cultivate, and empower these supporters to become your evangelists.

That requires training, teaching them how to use tools, and how to bring the message to others.

The goal of social networking is not to be a one-person show, but to create an army of people to take the message out.

According to Jeremiah Owyang, formerly of Forrester Research,[66] "An evangelist's role is to go beyond understanding and get others to believe in your product or service. This is beyond just communication and advertising and gets to the fundamental root of human communications, building trust."

People are many times more likely to take a friend's recommendation than a stranger's. Building an army of trusted friends will multiple your current efforts many fold.

---

[66] Quoted by Ashley Lomas: **bit.ly/8YRqmf**

The 10 Commandments of Social Computing

How to Engage with Social Computing

"Audience Engagement is the proportion
of visitors who participate in a specific
marketing initiative by contributing
comments, sharing or linking back"

Web Analytics DeMystified/Altimeter

The Holy Grail of social media is engagement. You'll see lots
of blogs, comments, studies, and other discussion on the
Internet about social media engagement. Everyone assumes
this is the highest goal one can achieve using social media,
because an engaged community is more likely to hear your
message, do what you request them to do, and in general hang
around and say nice things about you. But what actually is this
elusive thing: engagement?

What is Engagement?

Oddly, for a medium that talks a lot about improving engagement, there's not a lot of consensus on exactly what the term means. We present one definition — by two analyst firms, Web Analytics DeMystified and Altimeter — in the quote that begins this chapter, but it, like many definitions out there, actually seems to be more about defining the ways you can measure engagement than engagement itself. In their excellent report, *"The world's most valuable brands. Who's most engaged?"*[67] Altimeter joins with fellow analyst firm Wetpaint to measure major brands' level of social media engagement. Not once is the concept explained or defined. They obviously expect their audience of brand marketers to implicitly understand the term.

They're not alone. Lots of other really smart social media folks also seem to think engagement is merely a way to measure success. Lee Odden, online marketing and search engine master at Top Rank Online Marketing, says:

> Linking, bookmarking, blogging, referring, clicking, friending, connecting, subscribing, submitting inquiry forms and buying are all engagement measures at various points in the customer relationship.[68]

With all due respect to Odden's enormous expertise, blogging is a measure? We think it's an activity. That engaged people do.

---

[67] bit.ly/csCU4K

[68] Quoted by Jason Falls: bit.ly/bhqZbg

Others talk about the rewards enterprises can reap from the engaged. Social media guru Brian Solis points to statistics about engagement's effects on sales: "An impressive 51 percent of Facebook fans and 67 percent of Twitter followers indicated that they are more likely to buy since connecting online."[69]

Along these same lines, social media expert Jason Falls simplifies the definition, but perhaps a little too much: "Did you get something from your audience that can make your business better?"

Online community expert Amber Naslund gets a bit more specific, and a bit closer to an actual definition of engagement, saying[70] it involves one or all of the following:

- Interaction with unselfish intent
- Conversation
- Acknowledgement that we've been heard
- Responsiveness
- Unique contributions
- Personalized connection

The rest of the definitions we've seen run from the simplistic, and not all that helpful ("Conversing with others online in public and branded spaces" for example)[71] to lists of things to do to engage your community (provide high-quality content,

---

[69] bit.ly/djsMvj

[70] Amber Naslund runs social monitoring company Radian6's online communities: bit.ly/9ax9pM

[71] SayItSocial, who define themselves as Social Engagement Consultants: bit.ly/bD6b3j

answer questions, participate in conversations, provide great customer service to customers and potential customers, go off-line, meet in person).[72]

We don't really mean to tweak all these experts, but it is a sign of the new and maturing nature of social computing that so many talk about engagement, but so few attempt to define exactly what the term means. Apparently it's like art: We can't define it, but we know it when we see it.

We define social media engagement as interacting with a community that is:

- Listening
- Trusting
- Responding
- Communicating
- Acting

They are listening to you, maybe not all the time, but regularly or periodically. They trust what you say because you've built a rapport and a relationship with them. They respond to you, either by means of comments or other online participation, or by telling others about you. They are communicating their concerns, needs, passions, and interests to you; thus you can know them better. And, most importantly, they are acting. They may be buying your products, telling other about them, commenting, recommending, rating, or taking any of the myriad of actions you provide for them to get involved.

If your community is doing these things, they are engaged. And that's pretty much all you need to know about that.

---

[72] In a post entitled, ironically, "Six Ways to Define Social Media Engagement": **bit.ly/aReh54**

Joining the Conversation

As we've seen in earlier chapters, if you're a company of any size with sufficient history, people are already talking about you.

Do you ignore the conversation?

Or join in?

Well, if you've read this far, we hope you've decided that ignoring is not smart, and joining in is a real possibility. Let's talk about how you engage those who are talking about you or your enterprise.

Social Media Performance Group Social Media Approach

You'll find lots of prescriptions for social media success out there on the social Web, and many of them are known by snappy acronyms: The Five A's, the Four C's, 5x6, and so on. We couldn't come up with a slick acronym; didn't really try. What we have are five action verbs for execution (FAVEs? Oops. That one just sort of happened!) that you should keep in mind as you begin to engage with your community.

Here are the FAVEs in short, and we detail each of these in full version of **Be a Person**.

Listen

This one's first for a reason. Many businesses forget that you must listen before you speak. You must offer before you take. You must engage before you ask for action. Spend the first month or more of your social computing engagement process just listening to what people are saying. Restrain yourself from responding, even (especially!) if you see things you don't like.

Gauge the tenor of the conversation. What words do they use? How are they feeling? What gets them upset? What goads them to action?

During this phase, follow the old adage: It is better to be silent and thought a fool than to open your mouth and remove all doubt.

While you're listening, start sorting your community into segments. Who are the loudmouths? Who are respected? Who are emotional about your product? Who are skeptical?

You'll want to devise different approaches to the groups you find. The beauty of social computing is it enables you to address different groups differently. Start planning your engagement strategy while you listen. We talk more about listening in the chapter *Listen to Your Community* in the full version of **Be a Person**.

Find

OK this one logically comes first. How can you listen until you find who's speaking? But we think you see why Listen has to come first.

Mark Zuckerberg, the young creator of Facebook, famously said, "Communities already exist. Instead, think about how you can help that community do what it wants to do."

There's a community out there talking about you or your business. You need to find it and engage with it. Help it do what it wants to do. You probably won't have to look hard, but you should realize the community may exist only online, only offline, or both. If it's only offline, you've got a bit of convincing to do to get them online.

To find your community, ask around. Ask others in your field.

Google your business, products, product category. We've got more ideas in the *Find Your Community* section in the full version of **Be a Person**.

Engage

Engaging with your community means — at last! — joining the ongoing conversation. Don't think that you can land like a ton of bricks and start dominating. Follow the 4-to-1 rule: Comment on four posts for every post that you write. Give — invest — in the relationship before you ask for anything.

A great personal example of the need for giving before getting came after we did a seminar for a job seekers' group. After the presentation, an engineer came up to us and said, "LinkedIn doesn't work for job search." We asked why he thought this. "Well," he said, "I did what you said and joined the same LinkedIn group as someone who worked at my target company. I sent her a connection request, and she accepted. So I sent her a message asking her to introduce me to the hiring manager. And she refused! When I asked why, she said, 'I don't know you.' So LinkedIn doesn't work."

So what our engineer friend didn't realize, and what you need to always keep in mind, is that it's **social** networking. Approach it as you would approach building a relationship in real life. You may be able to meet more people online, but they're still people, and will develop a relationship with you over time, not immediately.

Once you have the hang of participating, you can begin to be more active — starting topics, offering more information about your business — but until your community is comfortable with you, don't get too heavy. Your early aim is to get people to check out your Website.

Which means you're probably going to need to renovate your

Website. You need to make it social-media-aware and social-media-friendly. We talk about some ways to do that in the section *Engagement on Your Site* and we get more detailed about engaging in the section *Engage Your Community* in the full version of **Be a Person**.

Ask

After you've earned your stripes with your community, you can start asking for action. Your first Ask shouldn't be as bold as, "By our product," or "Give us your number and a sales person will call." You've just met these people! It would be like arriving at a party in a beautiful mansion and asking, "So how much did you pay for this dump, anyway?" You could say that to your best friend, but you aren't best friends with your community yet.

Make sure your Ask is appropriate to the reputation and amount of social capital you've amassed through your participation. By no means should you immediately set up your own community and ask everyone to join. That step comes later, much later, if ever, and you'll probably know when it's appropriate.

Nonetheless, there's no harm in having lots of Asks on your existing site, and inviting your community to come by for a look. If people want to take an action, you need to make it easy for them. We explore asking in the section *Ask for the Commitment* in the full version of **Be a Person**.

Measure

You'll read a lot about social computing measurement on the Web. It's an obsession among certain people, many of whom swear it's not possible to measure social media outcomes.

We think social media is the only medium where it is possible to measure outcomes exactly.

You'll hear people claim, "I know exactly how much money I'll raise if I do this direct mail campaign." And they may be right. Through trial and error, they've discovered an approach that works. But can they tell you which of their messages go immediately into recycling? No, because if they could, they wouldn't mail those pieces out in the first place.

It's the same with TV and radio advertising. It's an old saw in the advertising world: "I know half of what I spend on advertising is wasted. I just don't know which half." Heh. Not really that funny considering you're talking blithely about wasting more than $209 billion annually in the US alone.

Online you can connect your actions with the response. Don't let anyone tell you any differently. It may not be a snap to do, but it's possible. We discuss how in the *Measure Results* section in the full version of **Be a Person**.

Where to Go from Here

Each of these components of our social media approach is further explained in the full version of **Be a Person**. Also in that volume is a wealth of how-to advice and tactics for creating your presence on popular social media sites, including the following chapters:

- Setting Up LinkedIn
- Setting Up Twitter
- Setting Up Facebook
- Setting Up YouTube for Non-Profits
- Setting Up MySpace
- Setting Up Blogging
- Building Your Community
- Community Building Checklist

You can find information about the full version of **Be a Person** on the Social Media Performance Group Website at: **bit.ly/gd0FTK**

Afterword

"It's only when technology gets boring —
that's to say, part of the routine for the
majority, not just the Geekosphere — that
it becomes interesting."

Clay Shirky

Well, that's it. A quick overview of everything you need to build your social presence online — Fast!

Because social media is so fast-moving, lots of the details in this book will rapidly become obsolete, perhaps by the time you read this. But the overarching concepts, we feel, will survive the constantly changing details. The sites may change; new capabilities may emerge; and certainly some new bright shiny thing will unseat the current 400-pound social media gorillas (we're looking at you, Facebook!)

But people don't change — basically — over the eons. Aristotle's two driving human attributes — pity and fear — remain alive in reality shows and gawker Websites, and the ways we relate to each other are as old as the hills.

We hope we've made some sense of this onrushing phenomenon, and we flatter ourselves to hope the advice in this book will remain relevant no matter how social computing evolves.

We'd like to hear from you, not only about what you think of our advice, but what you learn as you create your own social media practice. You can contribute by commenting on the Social Media Performance Group's Website at

www.SocialMediaPerformanceGroup.com

Be careful out there and remember, Don't Panic!

Who is the Social Media Performance Group?

The three principals of SMPG have varied and complementary capabilities and experience. We also partner with world class marketing, branding, design, and development resources to offer complete strategy-to-execution services.

Mike Ellsworth

Mike's background includes experience as an IT Program Manager, Chief Technology Officer for a start-up, Vice President of Strategic Planning for an Internet incubator, Senior Project Manager at the Nielsen Company, and as an independent Emerging Technology Strategy Consultant. During his 15-year career at the Nielsen Company in the marketing research business, he helped set Dun & Bradstreet's Internet strategy and developed the vision that resulted in the consumer packaged goods industry's first Web application in early 1995. With his own company, StratVantage Consulting, Mike helped Sterling Commerce create their eCommerce strategy and has helped senior leaders understand and connect rapidly changing new technologies with the organization's existing strategy.

In addition to starting StratVantage, Mike founded CTOMentor, a subscription-based emerging technology advisory service, and The WiMAX Guys, a wireless networking company. Most recently he leveraged more than a decade of social media experience (his first social media proposal was in

2001) by starting Linked InSolutions, a social media training and consulting company.

Ken Morris, JD

In addition to being a founding principal of SMPG, Ken is President and CEO of Aperçu Group Inc., a team of leading scholars and practitioners dedicated to helping organizations improve their financial and operational performance. In addition to social media consulting, Ken consults and coaches on issues of diversity, leadership, conflict management, succession planning, crisis management, team building, negotiation, presentation skills, workplace systems design, marketing, and strategic planning.

Ken's accomplishments include helping improve his customers' financial and operational performance; eCommerce and technology integration; Internet, intranet, networking and information technology; recruitment and retention; business and human resources strategy and execution; marketing and business development; international affairs; executive development, education and training; and community and governmental affairs.

Ken is a former Vice President of Human Resources at Boston Scientific and Guidant, Vice President, Business Development at Professional Development Group, Inc., and previously held positions at Honeywell and State Farm.

Robbie Johnson

Robbie is an experienced business development manager who has used social media in an innovative way to effectively connect with customers and prospects while driving sales performance. He has worked as Application Sales Representative and Business Development Consultant at Oracle before taking a business development role at Trissential, a Twin Cities IT solutions company. At Trissential, he landed three new customers, including Cargill, and $500,000 in new business solely through the use of social media techniques. In addition, he managed all of Trissential's partner relationships, including with Computer Associates, Oracle, Fujitsu, and others. As a result, Robbie helped Trissential grow from $6 million to $12 million in revenue during tough economic times.

Most recently, Robbie has leveraged his social networking strategy and execution experience to found Strategy Blueprints, a consulting firm that helps companies ensure that their tactical business plans map to their strategic business objectives, especially in the area of social networking and new media.

Acknowledgements

The editing and finishing of this book was an exercise in crowdsourcing. We are grateful for the assistance of the following reviewers, many of whom responded to our LinkedIn Question, who substantially improved this edition as well as the full edition of **Be a Person**:

Laura Bellinger — marketing communications producer and social media coordinator at Care USA. Laura launched CARE's social media and previously worked for CARE as a press officer. linkd.in/eT2qZH

Kari Carlisle — writer, archaeologist, museum curator for Fremont Indian State Park and Museum in central Utah where she cares for more than 150,000 artifacts; manages the park's archaeological sites, exhibits, educational programs, and special events; serves on the board of the Utah Museums Association; and chairs the committee for Richfield, Utah's annual Natural Resource Festival. linkd.in/eLZ52m

Robin Cheung — principal at Cloud 5 Nines.ca. Robin has been a pithy onliner ever since he was first introduced to it in 1987, he holds an MBA from McMaster University (Hamilton); showing his confidence in the future of the Internet, he is currently pursuing his PhD in Applied Management and Decision Sciences (Finance) from Walden University and maintains a business research and education blog at robincheung.ca/. linkd.in/hMhCFt

Barry Doctor — Product Marketing Manager at Katun Corporation. linkd.in/hVvkWo

Deb Ellsworth — creator of the Empathy Symbol, author of the novel, *Earth Portal,* and co-author of *Your Amazing Preschooler.* empathysymbol.com

Rob Etten — Vice President at The North Highland Company, Rob has experience with Ernst & Young's Management Consulting practice, Price Waterhouse, and Andersen Consulting (now Accenture). His areas of expertise include strategic planning, portfolio management, PMO startup, business process reengineering and merger/acquisition integration. linkd.in/hE3sV4

Roger Hamm — an experienced retail / CPG IT professional with expertise in Project Management, Implementation, Product Design and Principal at Viking Business Intelligence Services. linkd.in/hSKXmj

Dave Harkins — has helped lead change for nearly 25 years. His background includes extensive experience in marketing strategy, database marketing and direct response, branding, licensing and trademark management, marketing technology, and business development. He's served as VP, Strategic Services at the Jackson Group/Total Response, Managing Partner of Taylor-Harkins Group, Executive VP at Colman Brohan Davis, Chief Marketing Officer and VP, Customer Care at Geneer and VP, Marketing and Product Development at Nykamp Consulting Group. bit.ly/mi2dxo

Julie Kendrick — a features writer with a background in Web content development, magazine profiles and marketing communications. She is a contributing writer for minneapolispicks.com, alumni publications including Reach (U of MN alumni magazine) and Teton Thunder (Williston State College) and under contract to provide content and communications for Syngenta, a $12 billion global agricultural company. linkd.in/ifveBu

Trevor Lobel — project manager at Oswald Brothers. Trevor is a seasoned project and change manager experienced in software implementations for non-profit organizations and NGOs. linkd.in/fzdZxc

Tom Menke — a knowledge management professional known for his ability to leverage technologies, improve business processes, and work with people to improve staff collaboration and client communications to foster the sharing of knowledge and best practices. Tom was formerly Director of Knowledge Management at The Nielsen Company. linkd.in/fkb0Yu

Kathy Pettiss — science educator, consultant at Chester County (PA) Intermediate Unit and volunteer StarLab educator at Great Valley School District. linkd.in/efEkQc

Paul Phillips — Vice President of Operations at ACORN Research, LLC.

Paul serves on the board of the non-profit, HopeWorks (www.whyhopeworks.org) and is a published author. linkd.in/gSl9vl

Frances Ponick — principal at Ponick Enterprises. Frances specializes in writing, manuscript evaluation, book doctoring, and training book coaches. Frances has more than 30 years' experience in technical, business, marketing, proposal, and other nonfiction writing, editing, and publishing and has received awards for technical writing, journalism, and formal poetry. Frances worked at a nonprofit for ten years, and has taken graduate coursework on social marketing. www.franponick.com linkd.in/gfTCaj

ShaRon Rea — board member at the Harp Foundation and Hope Village Arizona. ShaRon is passionate about building strong community relationships. She is a motivator who believes in possibilities! linkd.in/hTXhqz

Mark Rieger — Vice President, Channel Maketing Evangelist for ChannelLine, which helps Technology Companies increase sales through a combination of consulting, research and the industry's only Pay For Performance demand generation program. linkd.in/gvkjM5

Alex Rodriguez — marketing director of Baywood Learning Center, a non-profit specializing in the education of gifted children. His many years working at and consulting with non-profits also include working at Trust for Public Land returning and reserving lands and parks for the public and Web consulting for non-profit Cacep. linkd.in/fXnvHO

Kathy Rose — a market research, shopper insights, consumer insights professional and principal of Rose Research for Results. linkd.in/gn61OB

Anthony Sansone — Senior Technical Editor at EMC Corporation. linkd.in/iku6vH

Leanne Storch — Associate Vice President, Pulmonary Fibrosis Foundation. Leanne brings organizational skills and a great empathy to the patients and families who call for support. linkd.in/eLACSO

Acknowledgements

The Best of the Best Pundits

These people inspired much of the thinking in this book. They really know their stuff.

Pundit	Link
Adam Christensen	bit.ly/cglyfw
Amber Naslund	bit.ly/aI4Ne6
Barry Judge	bit.ly/b6H0hY
Beth Kanter	bit.ly/dmp97X
Brian Solis	bit.ly/d8JMJb
Charlene Li	bit.ly/bV80w5
Chris Brogan	bit.ly/cXHzNA
Clay Shirky	bit.ly/dy9p2j
Guy Kawasaki	bit.ly/aUJB5m
Jason Falls	bit.ly/kuWUYT
Jeremiah Owyang	bit.ly/9aszgM

Pundit	Link
Josh Bernoff (Forrester Research)	bit.ly/a3ndiq
Katie Paine	bit.ly/982jqM
Lisa Barone	bit.ly/ivVfWU
Lee Odden	bit.ly/cQNLKG
Neal Schaffer	bit.ly/9GtQT4
Rachel Happe	bit.ly/blJkdb
Rick Mahn	bit.ly/aXmSdw
Dan Schwable	bit.ly/d3Zuyt
Robert Scoble	scoble.it/9NMNyh
Ron Shulkin	bit.ly/jHXgAh
Seth Godin	bit.ly/bdDjWc
Shel Israel	bit.ly/bgr9cM
The Cluetrain Team	bit.ly/9jGP3T

Everything you need to build your enterprise's social presence online — *Fast!*

Get the Full Version of Be a Person

More than 400 pages of strategy, tactics, and how-to information you can use to build your online social presence. Purchasing the book also includes:

- Gold access to the Social Media Performance Group online community

- One year of updated information as it becomes available

- Web access to the Enterprise Social Media Framework, which contains more than 50 case studies and dozens of social media best practices

Now taking orders for the print-on-demand or the Kindle version. See **bit.ly/gd0FTK** for more information

Visit the

SOCIAL MEDIA HALL OF SHAME!

SEE RANK SOCK PUPPETRY!!!

THRILL TO EMBARRASSING GOOFS BY OPRAH AND KFC!!!

GASP AT THE WRATH OF THE MOMMIE BLOGGERS!!!

But, seriously, take a tip from Thomas Edison—who said about his attempts to create the light bulb, "I have not failed. I've just found 10,000 ways that won't work"— and check out some of the things **not** to do with social media.

We include many of the 10,000 social media failures in our Social Media Hall of Shame from organizations who should know better, like Wal-Mart, Nestlé, Motrin, and the US Government.

Help avoid your own moments of shame by visiting the Hall at: **bit.ly/bjon3u**

You'll be glad you did!